coasting
a year by the bay

Also by

SUSAN KUROSAWA
in Sceptre

Places in the Heart

coasting
a year by the bay

SUSAN KUROSAWA

illustrations by Helen McCosker

An Alison Pressley Book

∫

SCEPTRE

A Sceptre Book

First published in Australia and New Zealand in 1999
by Hodder Headline Australia Pty Limited
(A member of the Hodder Headline Group)
Level 22, 201 Kent Street, Sydney NSW 2000
Website: www.hha.com.au

This paperback edition published in 2000

Published in association with Belladonna Books
39 Palmer Street, Balmain NSW 2041

Text copyright © Susan Kurosawa, 1999
Illustrations copyright © Helen McCosker, 1999

This book is copyright. Apart from any fair dealing for
the purposes of private study, research, criticism or
review as permitted under the *Copyright Act 1968*, no part
may be stored or reproduced by any process without
prior written permission. Enquiries should be made to the publisher.

National Library of Australia Cataloguing-in-Publication data

Kurosawa, Susan.
Coasting : a year by the bay.

ISBN 0 7336 1237 7

1. Kurosawa, Susan—Anecdotes. 2. Blundell, Graeme—
Anecdotes. 3. Country life—New South Wales—Hardys Bay—
Humor. 4. Hardy's Bay (N.S.W.)—Anecdotes. I. McCosker,
Helen. II. Title.

994.420922

Front and back cover photographs © Andrew Thomasson,
reproduced by kind permission of the photographer

Cover and text design by Danielle Cairis
Typeset by Bookhouse Digital, Sydney
Printed in Australia by Griffin Press Pty Ltd, Adelaide

For Graeme, naturally

In memory of Michael Vanstone, 1951–1994

With special thanks to Mary McKinney

Assistance and encouragement greatly appreciated from Maisie Drysdale, Andrew Strachan, Diana Kershaw, Paul Arrowsmith and Paul Booth, Garry Deakes and Greg Scott, Jenni Cregan and Merv Clayton, John McKinney, Jill and Frank Mullens, Sybil Medley, Judy Nunn and Bruce Venables, André and Tracey Chouvin, Beryl Strom, Elaine Fry, Andrew Thomasson, David Farnham, Julia Gauci and, of course, my publisher, Alison Pressley, for her friendship and jovial persistence and Helen McCosker for wonderful illustrations, as ever.

CONTENTS

Maps viii–ix

Chapter One
Dances with Pelicans 1
Pelicans 8

Chapter Two
Peacock Cottage 18
Peacocks 28

Chapter Three
Bay Watching 42
Brush Turkeys 52

Chapter Four
Pioneers and Property Developers 71

Chapter Five
Green Peace 91

Chapter Six
Some of My Friends Have Beaks 108
Kookaburras 130

Chapter Seven
Fibrocitis 132
Holiday Home Survival Kit 154

CONTENTS

Chapter Eight
The Summer People 155

Chapter Nine
Hooray for Hardywood 173

Chapter Ten
A River Runs Through 193

Chapter Eleven
Bay of Plenty 206
Fishy Business 233

Chapter Twelve
Travel, She Wrote 234
The Road Ahead? 257

Bibliography 258

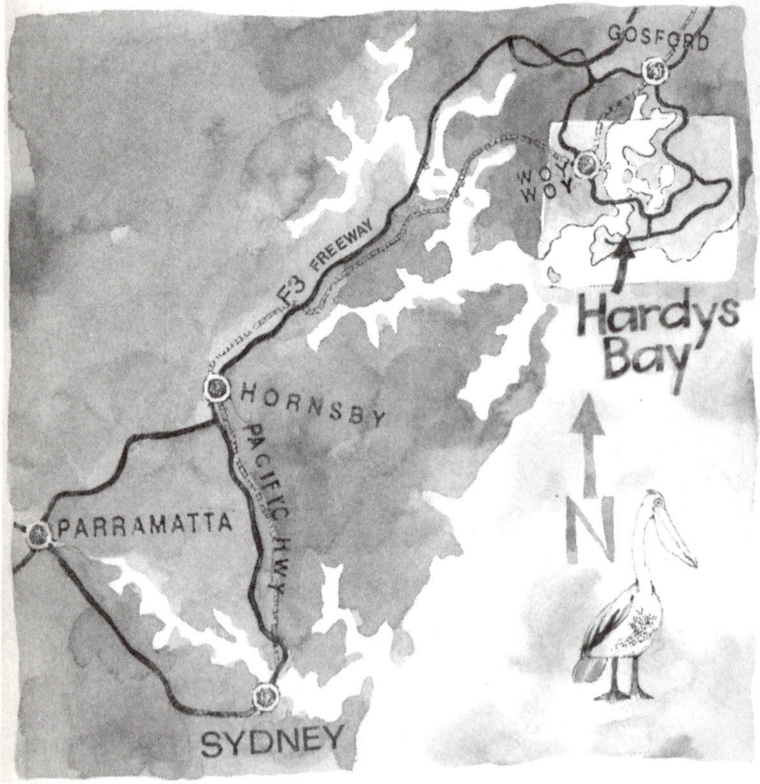
GOSFORD
WOY WOY
Hardys Bay
F3 FREEWAY
HORNSBY
PACIFIC HWY
PARRAMATTA
SYDNEY
N

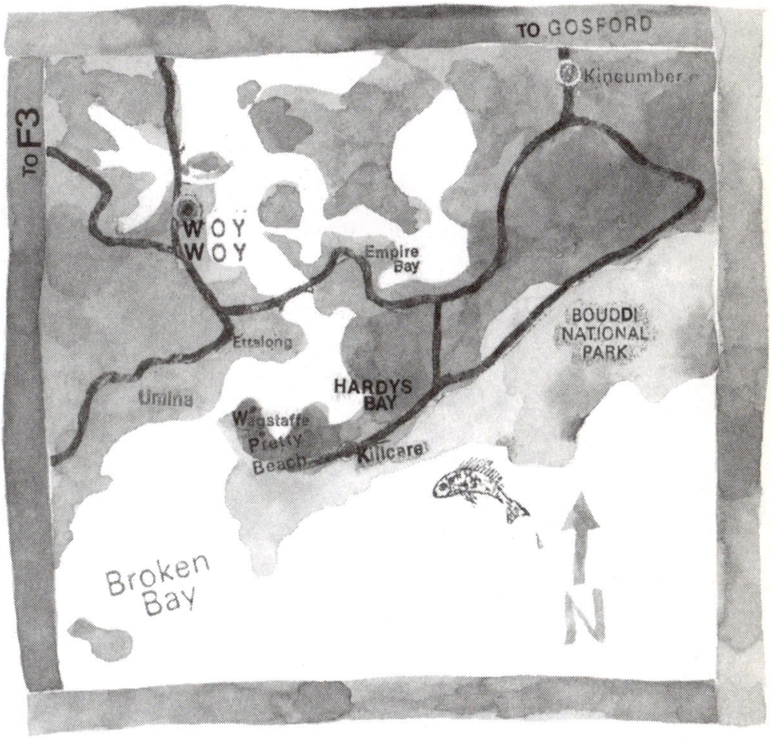
TO GOSFORD
Kincumber
To F3
WOY
WOY
Empire
Bay
Ettalong
BOUDDI
NATIONAL
PARK
HARDYS
BAY
Umina
Wagstaffe
Pretty
Beach
Killcare
Broken
Bay
N

CHAPTER ONE

Dances with Pelicans

'The pelican flew past us soon after we came to live in our house high on the bank... Now we wait uneasily if we miss his grave transit in the early morning, and wonder, are we late?'

Phyllis Albina Bennett

Let's blame the pelicans. As my partner, Graeme, and I drove down the hill toward Hardys Bay, a flight of six big-bellied birds flapped above us, as if hastily waved to centre-stage on an art director's cue. Grand pelicans, as dignified as undertakers. Seemingly too ungainly and heavy to fly, their presence enlarged the sky.

Later we would discover the pelican is emblematic of the New South Wales Central Coast, its improbable profile adorning postcards, logo brands, the hand-painted shingles of seaside guesthouses. But that day two years ago, the appearance of those birds at that precise moment seemed prophetic. We were escaping Sydney's inner west, driven out by endless planes bound for Mascot Airport. In our noise-induced paranoia, we imagined the jumbo jets using our terrace-house rooftop as an alignment point for their final approach.

Ninety minutes north of the city and here was a squadron of pelicans, in fighter-pilot formation, their only sound a stately swish of wings. We stopped the car and looked ahead. A big blue-glazed basin of water, beautifully proportioned, like an amphitheatre. Sailing boats bobbing at anchor and cabin cruisers moored beside a wooden jetty. Frangipanis and oleanders in profusion—later we would learn the poisonous but decorative 'ollies' had been planted in vast numbers because they were the only vegetation that cows on the pioneer selections wouldn't up and eat.

The Old Killcare Store, verandah-posted and tin-roofed. Mary McKinney, local real estate agent—Mother Mary, Patron Saint of the Bay, as we would come to call her—standing outside her waterfront office, hand shielding her strong face from the sun, in her fist a hoop of jangling keys worthy of a warden.

We explained to Mary we wanted a modest week-ender with views of the water, had to be fibro or wood, must come with a garden. And with something very Aussie about it, like a rainwater tank. Or an outdoor dunny. But not really a dunny that one had to use, I quickly added. All for less than a couple of hundred thousand dollars, we told her, sheepishly.

Earlier we'd been looking at nearby Pearl Beach, the glamorously laid-back bowl of sea and sand that accommodates the well-heeled Palm Beach overflow each summer. Our friend Ken has a house there, built tall and square on stilts, with a thigh-firming number of twisting steps and, once you've huffed and puffed to the top, there are distant but broad views of the Pacific.

All the Pearl Beach streets are named for valuable stones such as opal, tourmaline, amethyst, jade and coral. The real-estate agent who showed us around was keen to offload brick houses in back-block cul-de-sacs. Homes with yellow-bubble glass in the front-door panels and tidily grassed lawns with no fences. Like the satellite suburbs of Canberra transplanted to the coast, we decided. The Pearl Beach seafront strand with its designer houses of glass walls and horizon-searching belvederes was beyond our budget. We wondered if the agent had a Costume Jewellery Crescent or Plastic Place up his sleeve to show to blow-ins such as us.

We were all set to head back to Sydney when I remembered that another friend, Antonia, had mentioned Hardys Bay. The Pearl Beach salesman gave us Mary McKinney's number but not before telling us Hardys Bay was not known for its 'quality homes'. A call on my mobile phone to Mary who gave detailed directions, covering the roundabouts and sharp turns we would encounter—including a crucial swing to the left at the Ettalong Baptist Church with its hand-painted billboard ('Jesus the Carpenter is looking for Joiners').

She was still talking us in when we reached the crest of Killcare Road and were greeted by the welcoming committee of pelicans.

Into Mary's station-wagon for a sightseeing tour of Killcare, Hardys Bay, Pretty Beach and Wagstaffe. 'Do you want to look at ocean waves or ferry boats?' she asked of our preference in outlook. At Pearl Beach, we'd been made to feel we'd be lucky to buy a garage with a view of a fence with what we had to spend. Graeme and I looked at each other, unable to believe there could possibly be any such choice. 'Ferry boats,' we said, in unison.

We looked at three houses overlooking the Bay, which is what you come to call it within minutes, with the same easy informality that Port Douglas becomes just Port or New Orleans concertinas to Nawlins. The third, in the worst shape but with the most potential, was well within our price range but it had 'renovator's special' and 'handyman's delight' scrawled all over it.

Graeme and I sat on a rock on the cliff behind the house and drew up a mental list of pros and cons. On the plus side were the price and the location. Set one street back from the Bay, the house was elevated enough to allow water views over the lower rooftops. Unless Gosford City Council overturned all known zoning rules and a high-rise block of flats were to be built below, the panorama would never be blocked. The cliff stretched up to Bouddi National Park so there was no possibility of development behind us, either. In fact, the top of the ridge wasn't even visible through a variety of gums, some ghostly enough to look as if they could become animated by night, with branchy arms and legs like those in a children's pop-up story book.

The house had the archetypal architecture of a weekender. An almost square box, really, of white-painted timber, with a latticework skirt, reminiscent of the style of a Queenslander built on pylons to protect from floods and snakes. On the minus side was the state of the interior. As tiny as it was, the house had been partitioned into sleeping cubicles. Little kennels crammed with bunks, all stuffy and hot. Horrid old linoleum on the floor with a tracery of dirt and crushed shells. The bathroom was unusually big but badly designed, again with partitions, but these seemed to serve no purpose other than modesty panels. There was a grot of a shower recess in which bathers must have dumped Saharas of sand through the years. The kitchen was basic but rather cute with its shallow cupboards and battered old taps, exactly the plain but functional arrangement you'd expect in a holiday house.

On the plus side was its larrikin look. Cheekily lopsided, more lean-to extensions than haughty pretensions, unashamed of its absence of brick and tile. Under the house, an accumulation of summers past: a dinghy, inflatable beach toys with perished skins, broken fishing lines and worn nets, battered buckets and spades. Inside, cupboards bursting with unfashionable board games, jigsaws that we knew would be missing that final and crucial piece of sky, plastic bags jammed with mothy-looking Christmas decorations.

Mary told us the windows had come from an old Brisbane Water ferry-boat. Wood-framed, slightly irregular in shape and designed to slide clunkily along timber tracks. It was the sort of detail we'd been dreaming of. I imagined the place had been built by a retired sea captain who'd have looked out the eccentric little windows, scanning the horizon as if from a ship's bridge. 'It was originally used as a fishing cottage,' said Mary, as if to seal the deal.

'We'll get back to you,' I heard Graeme saying below. I had climbed further up the cliff, following the source of a mysterious rustle. Suddenly I was face-to-face with an Indian peafowl, a glorious blue male, his head tipped at an inquisitive angle. Pelicans overhead, a peacock in the garden, me who loved India, where the defining sound is the haunting screech of peacocks at dawn and dusk. I gasped, giddy-headed with the implications of it all.

'Wrap it up, Mary,' I yelled. 'We'll take it.'

•

I had always longed for a weekender. A crude cottage with water views, an uncomplicated place where I would be woken by birds, wear no shoes and sweep sand straight out the door. If I am to analyse this dream, I can see myself as a child, in England, with my parents, walking along the pebbled beach at Brighton, my hair worried by the wind, my skin itching beneath a woollen costume. Not an idyllic picture by sunny Australian standards, but to a five-year-old, the ocean and the seagulls and the fish and chips on the pier spelt holiday. And holidays were times when my parents stopped arguing, when my over-cautious mother went quite potty, allowing me to stay up past tea-time and eat ice-creams at any old hour. As for my father, he would put on his navy-blue swimming shorts with their odour of mothballs and run along the shore, while Mother and I sat in deckchairs rented by the hour and cheered him along as if he were training for an Olympic marathon.

In those days we'd stayed in boarding houses smelling of gravy and old-lady lavender. Later, when we settled in Sydney, via a beachless stint in Canberra, rented holiday cottages were the preferred option. Again, such escapes were times of great happiness, with all dental concerns put on hold as my father bought ice-blocks all round (Pipeline Petes were a particular favourite) and my mother served sugared Earl Grey and Iced Vo Vo biscuits at makeshift tea parties under moulting frangipani trees.

My family believed in lots of holidays, especially during the long summer school break. We'd plan our expeditions as if we were circumnavigating Australia. Mostly, though, we just drove to Avalon Beach, less than two hours away from our home in red-roofed Parramatta in Sydney's west, with all the trappings of safari stuffed in the Holden's boot. We'd install ourselves

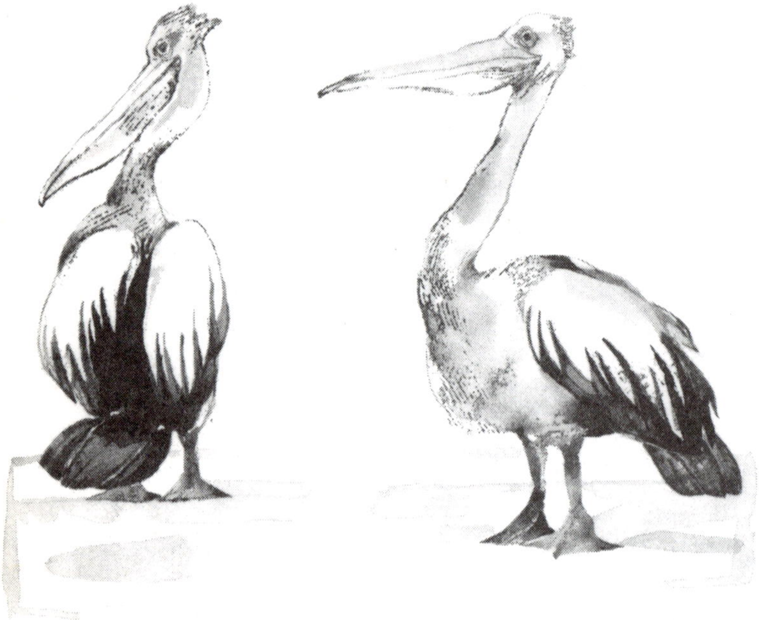

Pelicans

The species of pelican found in Australia is mostly white, with black markings. It's our largest water bird and is often seen flying with a flock, in formation; such a dark moving mass is thought to drive fish to the shallows where they can be easily plucked. When they land, pelicans appear to brake and water-ski to a stop on their webbed feet and, given their size, they are remarkably graceful. The best places on the New South Wales Central Coast for pelican spotting are at The Entrance and around the Woy Woy public wharf where they perch atop street lights, jetty posts and roofs.

There's organised pelican feeding at seaside Memorial Park at The Entrance every day from 3.30 p.m.; it's a practice which started years ago when employees of what was then the Clifford Fish Shop threw food to the birds. Beside Fishermen's Wharf on The Boulevarde at Woy Woy, on most Saturday and Sunday afternoons Wildlife Animal Rescue and Care Society rangers conduct a feeding and informative talk and monitor the pelicans' health.

in the rented cottage and send postcards to the relatives (who never travelled anywhere and were constantly agog at our daring) to assure them we'd safely landed in foreign parts.

And there we'd be, sleeping in other people's beds, invading their bookshelves, wondering at the contents of their cupboards and once, in a tatty wooden house with a caged cocky, finding a copy of *Man* magazine at the bottom of a wardrobe and tut-tutting, with my mother, over its bosomy contents while we sipped smart new instant coffee from the stoneware cups she'd bleached and scoured. We found a book of cocktail recipes in that house, too, tucked on a shelf behind one of those home bars with vinyl-covered stools and collections of coasters and swizzle-sticks. My mother grabbed the gin and vermouth bottles by their throats and quoted Dorothy Parker to me as she sloshed away:

> *I like to have a martini*
> *Two at the very most.*
> *After three I'm under the table,*
> *After four I'm under the host.*

I was simultaneously thrilled and shocked at such abandon. Mother usually was all manners and morals but on holidays absolutely anything seemed possible. No wonder I longed with all my heart for summer to roll around.

But there was a downside, to do with tidying and polishing. Other people's houses meant other people's germs, thus much scrubbing was required, with me acting as dusting deputy under Mother's argus-eyed direction. I used to wonder at the canny luck of these property barons who were not only paid for our presence but got my mother thrown in as a free spring-cleaning contractor.

Frequently, Mother and I would take it upon ourselves to redesign what she called 'chop suey decorations', meaning we'd mix up displays of ornaments, breezily moving china kittens away from their mothers, and changing pictures about—it was the era of painted white horses thundering into the surf and mass-produced Hong Kong oils of sailing junks and sampans. There may still be beach house-owners up and down Sydney's northern beaches peninsula who remember us as poltergeist-like tenants who blew through, leaving piles of date-ordered *National Geographics* and the pine scent of disinfectant in our wake.

Every morning, we'd set off to spend at least half the day at the beach. My English woollen 'costume' was replaced by a Jantzen 'cossie' with a shirred front which gave the unfortunate effect of a concave chest and on my head would be anchored a bathing cap festooned with poodle-like rubber curls. My mother, although not fat, believed in the merits of step-ins, but at the seaside she'd cast elastic to the breeze and fairly float like an unbottled genie in her cossie with a floral pleated skirt.

She always seemed younger, less anxious, on the beach and we'd gang up on my father, splashing him with water as he hesitated at the edge of the surf or burying his feet with sand as he snoozed in the sun.

But frequently, I'd feel faint from lack of circulation caused by my straitjacket cossie and would lie on the sand atop a big fringed towel patterned with Mexican hats. I wore T-bar sandals that constantly required unbuckling and I longed for the freedom of thongs but they were banned in our house, the wearing of same being a sure indicator you were low-class. Not to mention that they splayed your toes and therefore no one would marry you.

We ate devon sandwiches with tomato sauce and drank tea from a thermos. Seaside fast food was a concept restricted to packets of Smiths Crisps, which came with a waxy blue paper twist of salt, and delicious scoops of ice-creams in flaky cones. My parents did all they could to divert my attention from boys at the beach. Not that any male ever noticed me or, if he did, would have been convulsed with laughter at my corseted appearance.

But no heed was paid to protecting my skin. I sunbaked all day with no creams or lotions save for a cake-icing swipe of zinc cream on my nose—a further ploy by my parents to deter any lust-ravaged youths. Sometimes, I'd apply a layer of my mother's coconut oil and we'd lie side by side, turning over occasionally, like rotisserie chickens. If we ate out on holidays (that is, away from the rented house, where Mother made complicated salads with coloured cocktail onions tossed through, like confetti), it would be at milk bars and there would be fish and chips, buttered white bread on a side plate, perhaps a milkshake in a metal container with a paper straw. If soft drinks were on the menu, I'd be allowed to choose from an array of fruity flavours but never cola which was decried by my mother as the work of the devil, by which she meant the Americans, the same aliens who'd introduced biros (she was a stickler for fountain pens and scented notepaper).

•

All this I explained to Graeme, in detail, as we celebrated the purchase of our Hardys Bay weekender with a lunch at Fishermen's Wharf by the water at nearby Woy Woy. He was dazed with the suddenness of it all, having only half-believed I was serious about the purchase. 'I thought we were going for a scenic drive,' he muttered, as I popped the champagne cork and filled our Pyrex tumblers. 'It was the pelicans,' I protested.

I'd chosen a fortuitous location for our celebration lunch. Fishermen's Wharf is well named: it really *is* located on a pier, set behind a briny-smelling seafood market. On the opposite side of the Woy Woy Channel sits the perfectly named Pelican Island and the birds' breeding grounds are nearby, their nests lined with seaweed, grass, leaves and feathers.

The decor at Fishermen's Wharf consists of sky-blue plastic chairs, fake terrazzo tabletops and plastic sheeting on the windows. You collect your own cutlery and tumblers, set the table and open your wine. All around us, as grave as sentries, pelicans sat on poles and lampposts and on the roof, looking like beach-toys that had been freshly inflated, rubber-stoppered and positioned. Graeme didn't believe they were real and fixed the closest one with a riveting eye to see if it moved, just like tourists try to make Buckingham Palace guards flinch. I began naming them, like Colin Thiele's Storm Boy with his Mr Proud, Mr Ponder and Mr Percival.

Months later, I bought a copy of Phyllis Albina Bennett's compendium of poetry, with its many observations of pelicans, and marvelled at the resonance. This acute examiner of detail was born in 1906. A driving force on the Central Coast arts scene, she wrote hundreds of poems on subjects large and small, from bushwalkers 'loaded like tramps' to Woy Woy seagulls—'bold intruders' as she so aptly described them.

Was she lunching, I wonder, at Fishermen's Wharf, when she wrote of pelicans 'sitting like gargoyles on the posts of the landing at the jetty's end', when she described 'wide pulsing wings' and a body 'like a stout loaded hull'? Perhaps, like me, she asked the waitress if she could feed the pelicans. Not cooked food from the table, of course, but raw fish, big and wet with tungsten-coloured eyes. The waitress brought a bucket and flung wide the window so I could throw the birds their lunch. In a wink, Mr Ponder had turned to Mr Greedy. As Graeme gulped the bubbly and wondered at my madness, my arm all but disappeared up into my elbow as cartoonish shell-pink beaks engulfed their fish takeaways.

He told me months later that I looked 12 years old at that moment as I giggled and danced about and tossed the fish and all the diners on Fishermen's Wharf stopped their eating and cheered me on. Whatever it was I so desperately sought to recapture, Graeme knew I had found it on the Coast.

•

Back in Sydney, the reality set in. We would have to spend tens of thousands of dollars to bring the weekender up to scratch. Firstly, it needed a sundeck. Built in the 1920s, an era when fresh air was rarely a consideration, there was no outdoor sitting or entertaining area save for a barbecue terrace cut into the cliff. Inside, those sardined partitions would have to go, the lino needed to be ripped up and the bathroom reconfigured. 'Rub it out and start again, my girl,' Mother would have remarked, drawing on a filter-tip.

But we didn't want to destroy the essential holiday feel of the place. Whatever renovations were done would have to be simple and in character. Polished floors, marine and bushland colours, a plain wooden deck with nautical wiring. Out came the interior design magazines and my sketch pad.

'I think we'll call it Peacock Cottage,' I said, idly. This chance remark was to spark weeks of heated debate. Melbourne-born Graeme was determined it was a 'shack' and only up-themselves Sydneysiders, he scoffed, would refer to a weekender as a cottage. But to me the word shack sounded like not much more than a lean-to hut.

In New Zealand they're called batches, a derivation of bachelor shacks. Weeks after our purchase at the Bay,

I wrote a newspaper column about the shack and the batch, spelling the latter in that style. In flowed a swag of letters from irate Kiwi expatriates pointing out it should be 'bach', a word I can only read with the Johann Sebastian pronunciation. In the South Island of New Zealand, 'crib' is used, and what a nurturing, nannyish word it is. I can imagine snug weekends buttoned up in a weatherboard crib, safe against wind, rain, crashing surf and barking mad neighbours—perhaps with Johann Sebastian's fugues playing full pelt.

In South Australia they are most definitely shacks, while in Victoria they are holiday houses. Writing in the *Adelaide Review*, Kerryn Goldsworthy pointed out that some Melburnians live slightly more luxuriously 'when on retreat in their beach houses than they do in their ordinary lives' and even buy new furniture for them. 'I ask you,' she spluttered, South Australian to the core. 'The makeshift and unadorned South Australian shack functions mainly as a projection of one's daggier, less anxious and more innocent self.' Beautifully put. But luckily Kerryn's piece appeared more than a year after the *Coasting* saga began. If it'd been on hand during our cottage-versus-shack stoush, I doubt I'd have played fair and shown it to Graeme.

CHAPTER TWO

Peacock Cottage

He is a monstrous peacock, and he waveth all the night
His languid tail above us, lit with myriad spots of light.

from 'The Indian Upon God' by W.B. Yeats

I was to win the shack-versus-cottage debate, mainly on the grounds of the bird's persistent presence and the fact that Peacock Shack had a preposterous ring to it. With plans drawn up by our architect, Cedric, we made our first acquaintance with Gosford City Council. There was a great deal of to-ing and fro-ing over the dangerous implications of horizontal deck railings upon which 'kiddies could climb and fling themselves off', as one Council officer put it.

But all around the Bay were houses with horizontal rails and rods on their attenuated decks. Wooden, wire, rope, metal. Barely a house built into hill or cliff could be found which didn't boast a sundeck poking out its head, like a rubbernecking socialite, for a better view. In the end Cedric, who has a weekender at Pearl Beach and seemed resigned to Council logic and unfazed by opposition, announced we would be proceeding, albeit according to 'coastal time'—that tensile concept ruled by mysterious things such as tides, when the fish are biting, if Chris at the nursery has remembered our order of lilly pillies and when Adam the Gardener is quite sure it's the right phase of the moon for a spot of drystone walling.

Michael the builder was recommended by our other Pearl Beach friend, Ken, and many would be the night we'd drink a toast to his trustworthiness and efficiency. He seemed doubly god-like to us because of our dealings with Pe'er, he of the dropped t's in his speech and a short-cut view of construction. While we'd been waiting for the Council to approve the deck, Pe'er (please pronounce as if you've been watching an episode of 'The Bill') had been hired to rip up the lino, tear down the partitions and lay the new cypress floor as, sadly, the original boards had been in no condition to restore.

He had come via a recommendation from our friends in the Blue Mountains west of Sydney, Barry and Carmel, who were using him for renovation work on their timber retirement cottage (there definitely are no shacks at Wentworth Falls). Things came unstuck in the Mountains at about the same time as in the Bay. Visions ran riot of the dazed Pe'er careering, in Frank Spencer fashion, between the two locales, leaving a trail of 'bother' in his wake. Barry and Graeme began exchanging progress reports by phone, late at night, their melancholy heightened by cheap red wine. A curious kind of one-upmanship occurred as the pair compared horror tales. Barry would try to gazump us with stories of French doors that refused to open, windows that creaked, a wooden floor that had developed waves.

We trumped Barry and Carmel in the end, however. One Saturday morning we drove up to the Bay to inspect the floor laid by Pe'er and his band of bumblers. We turned the key in what had been a set of rather fine 1920s glass-panelled doors Graeme had found at a recycling yard. But then Pe'er had cut them down to hang, chopping from the bottom only, instead of equal distance from above and below, so now the door handle was around our knees. 'Easily fixed!' said Graeme. And those were his last printable words for quite some time as once inside he tripped over a floorboard which had buckled to the size of a tsunami, Pe'er not being one to believe in seasoning the timber before laying it. Graeme flew clear across the main room, through the (luckily) open bathroom door and came to rest next to the shower recess.

Michael's men were called in to re-lay the floor and fix up Pe'er's attempts at amateur carpentry. Finally, Barry and Graeme were forced to admit they'd hired him as he was cheaper than other advertised tradesmen—no doubt because Pe'er had had another life back in London, selling dairy cows to vegans or crocodiles to fish farmers. We refused to pay his final account, a fanciful column of figures written in pencil on a ruled exercise book page. Totting up the hours he'd charged, he would have had to be working 20 hours a day for a month. I wrote a cheque for about one-third of the amount and enclosed a curt note to say his services were terminated. When I rang his mobile to tell him the money was on its way and I wanted a receipt, Pe'er's voice was low and conspiratorial. 'I can't talk now,' he whispered. 'I'm in church.'

'Probably attending the funeral of some poor homeowner,' remarked Graeme, still sporting a bandage on his right knee.

•

The deck went up in grand fashion. Very broad, sitting way off the ground and, from certain angles, almost as big as the cottage itself. From the right-hand corner, the view is of the entrance to the Bay, with the main pier stretching into the water like a taut finger. Ahead and to the left, the vista is filtered through the leaves of tall gums on the low side of the street. We stood up there the Saturday morning after Michael had completed it— on time, at cost and without timber tidal waves—and drank a toast. We were not to be alone for long. The peacock I'd seen the day we bought the cottage appeared behind us. We'd sighted him a few times since then but he'd always trotted back into the bushes if we tried to tempt him closer.

We stood aside and let him inspect the new deck. Judging by the proprietorial way in which he marched up and down, he was convinced we'd built it as a performance platform for him. He flew up on to the top railing, shook his feathers, gave an almighty screech and then opened his tail as coquettishly as a geisha might unfold her fan. 'Every peacock is persuaded that his own tail is the finest in the world,' wrote Bertrand Russell, with telling economy.

A couple of motorists stopped their cars and got out to watch him strutting along the railing, dipping his tail as if taking bows, turning every so often to admire his bulky presence reflected in the ferry-boat windows. The next project would be to find him a name. I had in mind something Indian but our house-painter, Eduardo, originally from Chile and an old friend of Graeme's, took matters in hand. 'His name...it is Alfredo,' Eduardo advised me with a Latin shoulder-shrug as I visited one afternoon to check the colours that he and his son, Alex, were using for the cottage interiors.

Because Eduardo was so sure about it, in that fatalistic Latin way, I put away my notions of naming the bird for famous rulers who'd sat upon the Peacock Throne of Mughal India. I'd had in mind Shah Jahan, who had the fabled Taj Mahal built as a memorial to love, or the fearsome-sounding Akbar the Great. The actual Peacock Throne, commissioned by the beauty-worshipping Shah Jahan, was of pure gold, topped by an enamel canopy. Above stood a peacock, his gold body inlaid with precious stones, a ruby adorning the breast from which hung a pear-shaped pearl. The peacock's blue-and-green tail-feathers were made from sapphires and emeralds.

So, Alfredo he has been ever since—although several locals have told us that once there was a peacock pair, Andrew and Susan, living on our hillside but the female was run over. I'm glad we didn't know that story earlier as the idea of calling Andrew Peacock for tea (mushy fruit, mostly, served in a plastic dish) seems pretty silly —as, on reflection, does summoning Shah Jahan.

Eduardo and Alex painted the house according to a selection of coastal tones devised by another friend, Briony, who rejoices in the title of colour consultant. I was sceptical of outside opinion at first as I had a clear vision of maritime blues and greens and the rinsed pinks and mauves of sweet-peas. But Briony also introduced a rainy blue-grey, and bleached yellows the colour of sand and dry grass. The interior walls had been lined with tongue-and-groove wood in vertical strips by Pe'er and company (and we still expect any one of the panels to pop out some day and clobber us on the head) and then were painted with Briony's pastels.

Ceilings were painted high-gloss white, with rows of halogen spotlights installed in the main room. Above the calico-covered day bed that Pe'er had built according to my design (no sign of collapse—yet) and over the two side-by-side singles in the tiny second bedroom, we fitted wall lights shaped like shells which gave a soft, scalloped glow. The bed linen, shower curtain and tableware all reflected a nautical theme, with everything from anchors to gulls. Graeme loves the notion of 'found objects' and he'd bring in driftwood, broken shells and pieces of old metal he'd dug up in the garden. Having inherited my mother's tidiness gene, I'd just as quickly throw them out, fibbing to him that I'd set them aside 'for the time being'.

I found basin plugs in Noosa topped with metal turtles and two wooden boat wall-hangings made from ferry planking. Every time Alfredo pressed his head against the windows, there'd be another eccentric flounce or falderal to inspect.

In the bathroom we fitted a basin painted and glazed by a potter friend, Brooke. She devised a pattern of fish and fleshy mermaids, blue with splashes of heliotrope, and scripted lines around the top from *A Midsummer Night's Dream*:

> *Since once I sat upon a promontory,*
> *and heard a mermaid on a dolphin's back*
> *uttering such dulcet and harmonious breath,*
> *that the rude sea grew civil at her song,*
> *and certain stars shot madly from their spheres*
> *to hear the sea-maid's music.*

Guests spend ages washing their hands, reading the Shakespearean verse and wondering, I'm sure, if Graeme and I haven't gone just a little bit barmy.

Later, Brooke painted a small wooden chair and old cupboard for us in a dreamy aquamarine, again with mermaids, and a spunky long-haired merman, and verses about swimming. She'd spent holidays at Pretty Beach and knew the Hardys Bay basin well; some of her pottery was on sale in the Old Killcare Store. This revelation happened over and over again: while we imagined ourselves as pioneer discoverers, so many of our Sydney friends had been visiting the Coast since childhood. Even Cedric had spent some time as a boy living at Pretty Beach, a short-pants student at the little school. In those days, before the Rip Bridge linked Woy Woy and Booker Bay with our side of Brisbane Water, the teacher had to row across from Ettalong and of course all the children prayed, if not for sharks, then at least for weather too stormy for a crossing.

Our ferry windows, although not particularly practical, lent such an eccentric air to Peacock Cottage that they were left intact. Louvres were put into the bathroom and a spot marked for a future skylight; plans were drawn up for concertina-style French doors to be installed to open on to the deck. These would be needed as much for easy access as ventilation—in those early days, we had to walk out the front door, which is actually on the side, and reach the deck by an exterior ramp.

Then the outside was painted in three shades of green, ranging from a bushland tone through a silvery-olive to the deepness of GI Lime Cordial. For window trims, we chose a comic-book green of the brightness often seen in Caribbean houses. In fact, Peacock Cottage is distinctly Caribbean in appearance with its crooked tilt and dead-square shape. The main difference is it's not a 'shotgun' house—a term used in Jamaica and Antigua, and I'm sure elsewhere in the Caribbean, for little houses with central hallways through which one could fire a gun from the front door and the bullet would fly straight out the back.

To further the Caribbean character, we installed wooden shutters in the two bedrooms—'siesta shutters' as I've heard them called in the Antilles. And we bought two old timber planter chairs with low-slung seats and extended arms. Apparently these were designed so the master of the house could rest his legs, one at a time, on each arm, while the servant removed his boots. Graeme took this to be a pretty unlikely scenario: instead, we found the broad flat arms useful for setting aside our books and balancing the obligatory mixed drink at sundown. While thus seated one evening, with Alfredo at my elbow, I read a line in a magazine advertisement that beautifully summed up the scene on Peacock Cottage's deck. 'Tomorrow's weather forecast,' it declared, 'is fine, mostly sunny, with occasional martinis.' It made me think of Mother all those years ago, mixing a martini from the cocktail book in a rented beach house at Avalon, letting me have an olive and laughing fit to burst as my face puckered at its bitterness.

The quintessential Australian houses at the Bay are the fibro bungs. 'What on earth's a bung?' asked Val, our friend from London, as we sat on the deck. 'Or fibro, for that matter!' she added. My explanations of Aussie beachside vernacular led to nostalgic stories about English girlhood holidays. Val knew in an instant what I was trying to recapture at the Bay. We sat in girlish shorts and old straw hats and talked about scampi-and-chips in waxed paper and pier-end fortune-tellers and rowboats rented by the hour, always with names like *Saucy Sue*, as another English-born friend, Jeff, would later remind me. All to do with a different seaside culture but, in their way, the universal talismans of middle-class childhood holidays.

The work on Peacock Cottage was by no means complete by that stage. The fixing of the floorboards required several visits by Michael and his men, including the employment of a couple of steel posts to press the wood back into place. Mother Mary was aghast that we hadn't used local tradesmen in the first instance and we felt we'd failed an important initiation test by bringing in our own labour by way of London's East End and Wentworth Falls. What's more, it had all backfired so horribly and we were seriously out of pocket.

Michael is from Umina, some 10 minutes away by car, but we realised that he was hardly a 'local' in Mother Mary's terms. Nevertheless, she was admiring of his deckwork. We gratefully accepted her advice on a floor polisher, hardly daring to reveal we were bringing up our carpenter friend, Phil, from Sydney's beachside Bondi, to build 'fish furniture'. Phil is a big, bluff

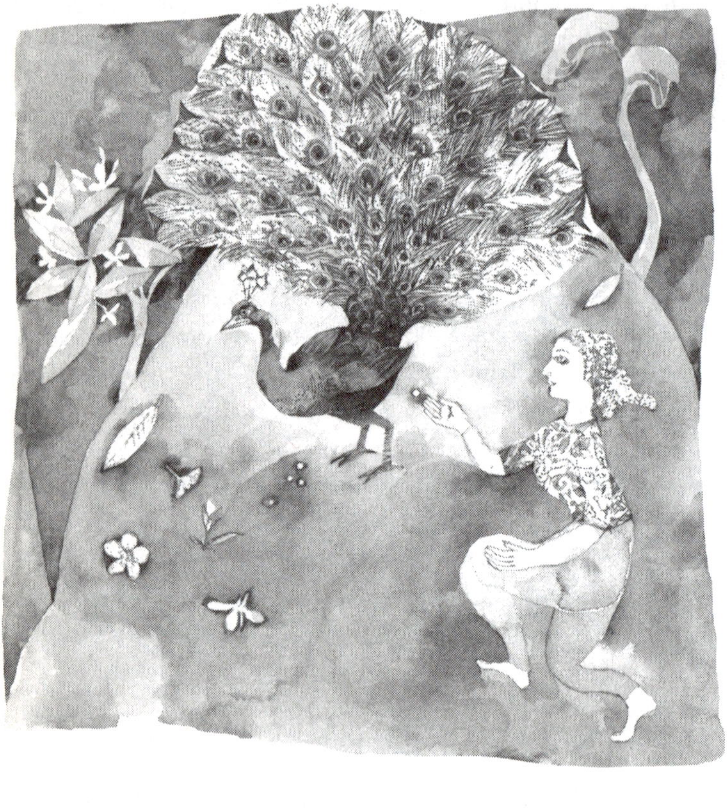

Peacocks

There's an ancient Chinese proverb that while other birds cry with jealousy at the rich and variegated plumage of the peacock, he is blushing at the sight of his ugly feet. John Ruskin observed that the most beautiful things in the world are the most useless—and he specifically cited lilies and peacocks.

The peacock is the national bird of India, consort of goddesses, protected by government statute and public sentiment. According to writer Nihal Mathur, 'Ancient Sanskrit texts celebrate the peacock as a symbol of joy.' Its joyousness is most apparent upon the breaking of the monsoon after months of heat and dust. 'In its resplendent plumage,' writes Mathur, 'it dances in gay abandon, welcoming the showers.'

The strident screech of the peacock is, to me, the defining sound of India. Mythology holds that the cry beckons to separated lovers to reunite, a constant stream through classical Indian music and dance and even pot-boiler Bollywood movies, where the appearance of a strutting peacock in full tail signifies, with modest allusion, the male actor's engorged desires.

Science writer Graeme Phillips takes a more contemporary tack. 'The males persist with the pointless plumage because it gets the girls,' he says. In short, Phillips cleverly dubs the peacock's tail 'an elaborate chick magnet'.

one-time cotton farmer from Moree with an artistic bent. Now he makes bespoke pieces from recycled timber, much of it with a beach-inspired theme complete with whimsical touches.

Next time Mother Mary stepped inside Peacock Cottage, she was greeted with wooden fish motifs on the new bathroom and toilet doors, fish swimming along the cross-supports of a round dining table and fish handles on drawers—the triangular tail makes an easy grip! Under the day bed, Phil had constructed cupboards, also with fish handles. But the pièce de résistance was a line of gaudy gold fish wriggling across the entranceway on the newly polished boards. Mother Mary looked at them in horror. And so did I. The day before, there'd been no fish on the floor, and the pattern didn't have the mark of Phil's handiwork. We found a note from Hans, the floor polisher, advising that he'd added a few more fish at no extra cost.

After his artistic triumph, Hans must have repaired to the Hardys Bay RSL and Citizens Club ('The Biggest Little Club on the Coast') for a reviving drink and a day's debriefing with his mates. Because by next day, Peacock Cottage was the talk of the Bay. The general consensus was that it was being got ready as headquarters for a Christian cult. 'Fish-worshippers!' was the muttered mantra.

We began to feel as if we'd pitched up in an episode of television's 'Hamish Macbeth' or 'Ballykissangel'. Here we were, the townie interlopers, coming in with our strange ways, upsetting the pattern of the place, trying to corrupt the good decent feel of the Bay with our Caribbean colours and Balinese day beds and fertility goddesses (that is, an Indonesian stone carving of a bare-breasted water-carrier which had also incited local interest).

Phil continued carving fish and building bookcases for us and we kept to ourselves as we tried to work out the logistics of our life. By now, Peacock Cottage was liveable and we'd started to bring up books and oddments of furniture from Sydney each weekend. But the attachment we were forming with the Bay had started to affect the otherwise smooth pattern of our lives. I wanted to go every weekend, Graeme sometimes preferred to stay in Sydney. There was his pre-teen daughter, Harriet, to consider, who came to us most weekends and played sport in winter, meaning Graeme's Saturdays had to be spent around a series of wind-whipped ovals in various Sydney suburbs.

Then there was the drive. I love driving but Graeme doesn't. During that period, I owned a Ford Capri convertible which I'd bought myself for my fortieth birthday. It was an important expression of my independence. My sons, Justin and Joe, had left home (for the first time, that is; they both have the migratory patterns of boomerangs) and I revelled in driving a car that fairly shrieked of unattachment—no room for a siege-like cargo of supermarket shopping bags, unwieldy sports gear (Justin's fencing épées and kendo fighting sticks, in particular) and gangs of junior rugby players, all built like fridges on legs.

I'd fly up the F3 Freeway which links Hornsby in Sydney's far north to Newcastle. Whip off at the Gosford entrance, along the twisting road through Kariong, belt down Blackwall Mountain, through Woy Woy, past Ettalong, St Huberts Island and Empire Bay and up Wards Hill Road. There's something quite mad about the way you have to turn back on yourself to reach the Bay, so close to Sydney as the crow flies, but a fair imitation of the looped ABC logo in terms of roads.

Just past the crest of Wards Hill Road, the first real glimpse of the ocean. And on sailing days, the waves tipped with whitecaps and yachts galore, looking like quick bright brushstrokes on a Ken Done sea. Down the hill to Hardys Bay, all in 90 minutes flat. Usually with the top down and the radio up. This prelude to a visit to the Bay was almost as enjoyable as the place itself. Whatever stresses I was carrying from the city and the office seemed to melt away as I ripped along.

Graeme is the ultimate urban animal. He'd moved from Melbourne 20 years earlier and all his Sydney time had been spent in inner-city terrace houses within cooee of Kings Cross. And I knew he disliked driving through the bush. Once past the Kariong turn-off, the landscape becomes very densely vegetated with gums and acacia and signs warning of kangaroos crossing. There's little sense of being near civilisation until a break in the trees reveals glistening seascapes with distant houses dotting the headlands, many of them pole homes set at treacherous angles, looking like ungainly wading birds poised for take-off.

We started to argue over how much time to spend at the Bay and Graeme was loath to ever drive up alone. The Capri was impractical for carrying anything except a carefree overnight bag but I didn't want to drive his car—a truck, practically—which almost required a stepladder for me to board. One night as we sat in the city surveying the accounts, including Michael's reminder invoice for the deck, I realised the Capri would have to go. Graeme accepted a little too readily my suggestion that I sell it and I went into a dark sulk. He had no idea just what the sportscar meant to someone who'd been married at 20, a mother at 21, again at 22, and whose sole experience of impetuous youth had been the two-year period between graduation and pregnancy.

But there was no other option and pretty soon we were calling the deck 'The Capri', as what I got for the car neatly paid Michael's bill. I got over my upset pretty soon although when my publisher, Alison, arrives these days at the Bay in her mid-life-crisis-on-wheels, a snappy little topless Mazda, I feel a horrible twinge of envy. We sorted out the vehicle situation by buying an urban cowgirl four-wheel-drive for me with enough space for Graeme and Harriet to be comfortable plus sufficient room in the back for loads of weekend supplies.

Graeme had traded-in his truck for the four-wheel-drive so we still needed a second vehicle. He decided that nothing less than a ute would suit his new feral incarnation. Not an accessorised pick-up sitting way off the ground in the style of those smart American models but a second-hand Toyota Hilux with a great tin tray out the back, a radio so old it picks up only AM stations (with what seems to be a permanent flip towards the footy and the cricket) and beige vinyl upholstery to which one adheres on a sticky day as if to fly-paper.

I surveyed the ute with a thin smile and asked him if he planned to drive it in public. He looked so crestfallen that I told him it wouldn't be so bad once I'd decorated it. Not exactly cafe curtains across the rear window or fluffy animals on the dash, but perhaps Country Road calico seat-covers and a retractable ladder into the passenger side of the cabin. As with his earlier truck, again there was the matter of mounting and dismounting. Being so short of leg, getting into the ute almost entailed for me a run-up and flying leap in the style of a pole vault. Once installed, I couldn't see over the dashboard, which seemed something of a disadvantage when it was my turn to drive.

Graeme reminded me that our first-ever kiss, in October 1995, had taken place in his old truck and I should maintain something of a soft spot for such vehicles. 'You melted in my arms,' he said. I didn't point out that was because I had slid on the sweaty vinyl and all but landed in his lap.

I gave him an enigmatic smile and presented him with a list of accessories for the modern ute owner. To wit: if the ute isn't dirty and dangerous-looking in the style of a proper workhorse, you can buy spray-on mud. To look like a real man on the land, the contemporary ute owner needs a blue heeler dog. To save time and maintenance, an inflatable one can be bought, especially designed with moulded paws that grip the back of the tray. The model with brake light eyes and a wobbling head costs extra.

Then there's the standard ute owner's tray display kit: assorted refuse (cans, chip wrappers, empty cardboard milkshake containers), mismatched tools, lengths of rope, torn tarpaulins and rusty wheelbarrow. Some enterprising retailer should bundle these essentials into one big package, ready to be unloaded onto the tray.

As part of Graeme's new beaut-ute image, he began wearing baggy shorts and singlets and grubby baseball caps. He's frequently hailed on the street by people who recognise him from films and television, so to escape detection, he took to pulling the caps way down. But then he just looked like Graeme Blundell in a funny hat. 'Gettin' any these days, Alvin?' asked a fisherman one afternoon as we walked along the Wagstaffe public wharf. '*Alvin Purple* was more than 25 years ago,' he muttered to me over his shoulder. I turned around and walked back, lest I be mistaken for Abigail gone to pot.

In his new Bay gear, he opened an account at a Woy Woy hardware barn, a place the size of an aircraft hangar with dress code definitely black or blue singlet. Thus attired, he decided he'd fraternise with the local tradesmen—the 'tradies'—and unlock the mysteries of the universe (or at least of shifting spanners and ball valves) over a convivial drink. They told him to meet them at Bar Otto.

Pretty swish name, we thought, for a watering hole in this, a one-pelican town. Where could it be? No clues at the RSL and Citizens Club and, in the absence of anywhere else to drink, he drifted towards a cluster of tinny-waving blokes at the Hardys Bay pier. Suddenly it all became clear. The alfresco bar was so named for the Council's big green Otto bins next to the public toilet. Strictly BYO and nothing but a six-pack from the bottle shop would do.

Shade at Bar Otto is provided by two spreading coral trees and Happy Hour at the Bay gets going at about 4.30 in the afternoon when the tradies knock off work. It works as an information exchange as well as a watering hole, with news swapped about local jobs and who might be in need of a sub-contractor. It's also known as the Office, for this reason, but Mother Mary calls it the Yum Yum tree and her two sons are regulars, along with such Bay characters as an almost-blind man who fairly flies along the waterfront on two white sticks as soon as he hears the afternoon's first crack of a ring-pull can. Things wind down at sunset in winter, maybe drifting a bit later on a balmy summer's evening, when pink-and-grey flocks of galahs wheel overhead and the lilting voice of Mother Mary can be heard across the Bay, calling her sons, Dylan and Joe, back home.

Pearl Beach used to have a Jewfish tree in the 1930s, so named because local fishermen would nail the heads of their biggest catches to its trunk, complete with a little note about the fish's weight. It was sited opposite the Pearl Beach Store, apparently a gruesome sight on a par with the guillotined heads on spikes of the French Revolution. Passers-by would have had to time their journey with some precision, according to the direction of the wind.

•

Now with two 'coastal cars', Graeme and I would often visit the Bay independently. I was travelling a lot, too, usually zipping overseas on newspaper assignments once a month. I always returned with not just a story but a loaded suitcase. The cottage became a showcase of my travels. Mostly, I hunted for marine themes, but my love of India and Bali overrode everything and the garden water-carrier statue was soon joined by rust-red Lombok pottery and stone fish and brilliant fabrics from Rajasthan. Rajahs riding elephants, Mughal emperors strolling through pleasure gardens, snooty camels caparisoned with tasselled finery—the cushions, loose chair covers and day-bed bolsters were a riot of colour and imagination.

A Mughal peacock motif on a large cushion propped at the end of the day bed by the window served as a mirror for Alfredo when he performed his pavonine passeggiata on the deck each evening. Judging by the preening that went on, he clearly imagined he was that very bird which had modelled for the jewel-encrusted Peacock Throne.

But the more I journeyed, the more homesick I became. And it was never a longing for suburban Sydney—always for the Bay. I worried about Alfredo and hoped he wasn't too lonely—his amorous advances toward the local brush turkeys were never reciprocated. If it was raining in the night in Delhi, I'd lie awake wondering if it was wet, too, at the Bay, and if Graeme's new subtropical plantings were drinking their fill.

On one such night, I rang Graeme and cried. I was in French Polynesia during a tropical storm and the line was bad. Our untethered voices were floating in space, disembodied and metallic, as if being synthesised as sound effects. 'We have to move to the Bay,' I said, with an echo, between sobs. I told him I couldn't bear the dual existence any longer, the running of two houses, the dreadful wrench I felt every time we drove out on Killcare Road with the Bay in the rear-vision mirror.

'It won't work,' he said, flatly, his voice blurry with sleep.

•

There were a hundred reasons why it could have been destined to failure. Firstly, we both worked—and still do—in the city. But our jobs are not structured according to nine-to-five office rules. Although I edit a newspaper section, I also write two weekly columns plus book reviews and other pieces across the paper. A day or two during the week to be spent writing at the Bay was not only feasible but eminently sensible, given the distractions and interruptions at the office. Graeme's working life was less structured and he often had to dash at short notice to a studio to record a voice-over for a radio or television commercial. He knew there was a stage role coming up later in the year for him in Sydney and a 90-minute commute in each direction would be intolerable.

Peacock Cottage was too small to be anything more than a casual weekender. We'd already jammed it with books and my caravanserai of artefacts. Phil was a regular visitor and he seemed to be purging all his creative frustrations by carving more and more fish into the surfaces. The only way to live permanently at the Bay was to buy a bigger house or extend Peacock Cottage, either by building a second storey or excavating into the cliff behind. And we'd still need a Sydney base.

Justin was living in a small converted warehouse apartment I'd bought several years earlier in Surry Hills. He was less than amused when I told him we were leaving our inner-west terrace and he was to be turfed out. Seven minutes walk from my office, the apartment was far too tiny to be a primary residence for Graeme and me but it would do perfectly as a pied-a-terre. Justin moved into a Woolloomooloo terrace with a work colleague and we had Cedric draw up some plans for phase two of Peacock Cottage.

As we repainted the Surry Hills apartment, there was bad news from our bank manager, Lyle. Losing Justin's rental income meant no negative gearing, which I badly needed for tax relief. He suggested we should rent out Peacock Cottage until the extension work was complete—which Cedric estimated would take a year, given his hair-tearing prior dealings with Gosford City Council.

A neat solution on paper but it meant we were cut off from the Bay. I turned to Mother Mary. She had several good houses on her books that we could rent—all of them big enough to cope with the overflow from our Sydney home. I drove up one morning and met Mother Mary's property manager, Kerrie, and within an hour I'd settled on a pale-blue house placed right on the water on the opposite side of the Bay to Peacock Cottage. I stood on its deck with my binoculars and realised I couldn't see our place but I could hear it. From behind a big, bosky clump, Alfredo was screeching his pretty blue head off.

That night, I told Graeme I'd taken a 12-month lease on a rather poky but not unattractive cottage. Its best point was an absolute water frontage with a wooden jetty and, behind, a hill clumped with bird-filled trees. 'What's the matter with it?' he asked, my description being altogether too good to be true.

'Its name,' I told him.

'Nothing could be sillier than Peacock Cottage,' he replied, woundingly.

I'm sure my voice carried a discernible note of triumph as I told him the sign on the front of our new temporary home said 'Thistle Do'.

CHAPTER THREE

Bay Watching

'Governor Phillip peered anxiously through the curtain of rain... He spent his first night in the Central Coast wet and uncomfortable aboard his whaleboat.'

from Brisbane Water Historical Society literature

Historians appear to disagree if Phillip's party was moored off Pearl Beach or Lobster Beach but there's consensus on the subject of a lashing deluge. To say it merely rained the day of our move, two centuries and a decade later, would be to call a pond a puddle. It poured, the wind whirled sheets of water in all directions, the removalist men wore oilskins and my tears of frustration added to the general dampness.

By mid-morning, Graeme had banished me to the office. I left him at the terrace-house door holding pages of my typed instructions. He looked like an air-traffic controller, ushering boxes and pieces of furniture into separate trucks, according to their destination. For days we'd been numbering and marking cartons and attaching tags to larger items. So tired and frazzled had we become that we almost sent all the beds to the Bay, leaving the Surry Hills bedrooms potentially bare.

Graeme drove the ute ahead of the truck bound for the Bay. The rain had become so heavy that progress was at turtle's pace. The tray of the ute was stacked with boxes, too, and its plastic cover sheet kept blowing up like a spinnaker. By the time he crossed the Mooney Mooney Bridge, he later told me, it was one of life's small miracles that he didn't become airborne and sail off down the Hawkesbury River.

That night when I met him back at the apartment, we hugged each other and cried. There were boxes everywhere and no room to move unless we walked sideways, like crabs. We'd severely overestimated the amount of space we'd have to store books so the night was spent moving most of the cartons onto the covered balcony. Graeme fell asleep on the unmade bed and we set the alarm clock for six as there was still another load to go by removalist van up to the Bay. I didn't tell him that Joe, the younger of my sons, had called me at the office from overseas to say he was coming 'home' at the end of the week.

'What have you done with my room!' wailed Joe as I met him at the airport and explained we weren't driving to 'his' four-bedroom terrace in Stanmore but to a two-bedroom closet in Surry Hills. But as he'd been living in Japan for a year, sleeping in a minuscule flat, the apartment seemed reasonably large to him, even though he remarked that the entire place could fit into the lounge-room of the Stanmore home.

At first, he intended to stay for just a few weeks but as is the way with single male offspring, he was there for a year. Happily, it worked out well as Graeme and I spent the bulk of each week at the Bay aside from the three-month period when he was appearing in the play 'Navigating' with his good friend Noni Hazlehurst at the Sydney Opera House.

During those extended periods at the Bay, I commuted to Central Station on the Newcastle Express, boarding at Woy Woy Station, surely one of Australia's most fortuitously sited, with its wide nautical views and water-skiers scooting parallel with the platforms. Even its design of porthole windows and sunny colours transcends the railway vernacular norm. An advertisement in the long-defunct *Walkabout* magazine in December 1958 boasted of 'The Scenic Northern Line' from Sydney to Gosford via Woy Woy. 'Air-conditioned Newcastle Expresses enable the tourist to see this picturesque portion of the State under the best conditions,' it read, with the added promise of 'extensive views of tree-clad hillsides'.

'This Month on the Central Coast', a free guide for visitors, reports that in 1918, at the start of the post-war holiday boom, tourists paid sixpence each to travel 'by motor service' from Woy Woy Station to Ettalong. I had my own chauffeur most evenings, albeit one in baseball cap and shorts. Graeme would collect me from the train under the 'Kiss and Ride' sign for the 15-minute drive to the Bay. Comedian Spike Milligan would no doubt approve of the Goon-like implications of such a civic sign; it was he who put Woy Woy on the map and has done as much for its reputation as Dame Edna Everage for Moonee Ponds. 'The world's only above-ground cemetery' he famously called Woy Woy while on a visit to his elderly parents in their fibro bung. Less well known is that Hardys Bay was known as 'the cemetery with lights' by the Ettalong and Woy Woy mob before the Rip Bridge, a direct lifeline across Brisbane Water, was opened in 1972.

As we buzzed back to the Bay, I'd entertain Graeme with stories of my fellow rail commuters, some of whom appeared to be barking mad. 'I am he in the car full of students celebrating victory with instruments saxophonic and ukulelean...' and 'He whom the argumentative tippler oozes in beside though there are thirty empty seats in the coach...' wrote poet Ogden Nash of his eventful travels by public conveyance. 'Never make eye contact,' our Wentworth Falls friend, Barry, had told me. By now he was a veteran of the long Blue Mountains-to-Sydney run and I had visions of him glued to his reading matter, too worried to manage even a sideways glance at what the carriage might hold.

Phyllis Albina Bennett was my chosen companion for the seventy-minute journey, her book of poems and prose always in my bag. One section is simply titled

'Commuter': the train tracks become 'glistening silver snakes', the exact composition of the bush described in meticulous detail. She imbued even the tunnels and the Hawkesbury River with Gothic mystery. She must have regularly caught a morning train, late enough to qualify for a cheaper, off-peak ticket. 'The 10.23 a.m. from Gosford' is the title of one long, blank verse. 'This is a melancholy train frequented by the old and broken. They dither and bumble along the corridors, looking not only for space but for the spaciousness of a more leisurely age,' she began.

After a few weeks, little routines emerged: always sit on the left-hand side going down the Coast, the opposite coming back, such positioning being necessary to take advantage of the best water views. The line coils around bays, whooshes through a series of tunnels, flies across the Hawkesbury courtesy of high, black bridges. Houses reached only by boat, all with wooden jetties, hunkered against sandstone hills, a nimbus of woodsmoke in winter. Oyster leases patterning the water like the linear design of a Mondrian canvas.

On days when the mists lie low and as wispy as organza, the waterways look like a series of Scottish lochs, brooding and enchanted, hiding places of monsters. 'The North East Arm of Broken Bay is one of the finest enclosed pieces of water in any colony,' announced *The Sydney Gazette* of June 16, 1825, 'resembling, it is said, in extent and smoothness the beautiful water of Loch Lomond.'

Close to the first real signs of civilisation, onwards from Berowra, the totems of suburbia appear. Hills Hoists billow with sheets, boronia and eucalyptus give way to manicured plots. Passengers peer into backyards, each telling its own story with stage props of children's plastic wading pools and swings, a kennel, a rabbit hutch, an onion-domed wooden gazebo dominating the grass like a sultan's folly, an old lady asleep in a wicker chair under a mulberry tree. But it's somehow wild, too, with fugitive kookaburras on the clothes lines and runaway jasmine on the banks. Next stop Hornsby, then Epping or Eastwood, depending on the timetable, always Strathfield and Central. Or City Terminal, as the guards call it, with an ominously final ring.

•

We had settled well into Thistle Do, filling it with our books. The garage was too crammed with unpacked boxes for either car to fit. We no longer knew what was inside those cartons, but all we could do was shrug and agree they weren't concealing anything essential to our existence. A once bunk-lined bedroom became my office. The owners seemed astonished we didn't actually want a house capable of accommodating people like battery-hens filed in bunks and it took Kerrie's full powers of persuasion to have the house emptied of holiday furniture for us. At the rear of Thistle Do, my cabin-style office had a view of the garden, not water and pelicans and other such beguiling distractions.

The contents of Peacock Cottage were scaled down so holiday tenants would have room to move. Phil had made tall bookcases carved, naturally, with fishy flourishes and we filled the shelves with a selection of books we thought renters might enjoy. In a perfect capsule of description, Logan Pearsall Smith wrote of reading, 'This polite unpunishable vice.' If owning too many books were a crime, Graeme and I would be serving life. We agonised over the final selection, determined to do better than the usual rental-cottage array of dog-eared *National Geographic*s and shelves of what author Margaret Atwood calls a 'koob'—a book-shaped object not deserving of the status of book as it contains no worthy reading.

Graeme is a crime fiction addict so plenty of 'blood boilers', as I call them, were placed in residence. Picture books (high-gloss 'koobs', actually) on topics from the mardi gras in New Orleans to the gardens of the French Riviera were placed on the coffee table and on a Balinese chest in the larger bedroom. I gathered a haul of Theroux, Newby, Raban, Thubron, Murphy, Morris and Bryson for a dedicated travel section and we added some 'cosies' in the form of Agatha Christie and Dorothy L. Sayers, plus anthologies and collections of short stories. A Maugham on the deck with a martini seemed the right recipe.

All was now painted, prinked, polished and preened. Bank manager Lyle ('the albatross' is how he chooses to describe himself) was insistent it had to be rented as soon as possible so we listed it with Mother Mary and waited for news of summer tenants.

It was then we discovered the 'Love me, love my kids' brigade. Even though the little brochure I'd concocted waxed lyrical about tranquillity and romantic cosiness and specifically mentioned that Peacock Cottage was on the side of a cliff and had dozens of steep steps, potential renters arrived with small, lively kids in tow. One good bout of watch-me-mummy-I'm-a-tightrope-walker and these small funsters would have been off the railings and hurtling down to the Bay before you could say Corky the Clown.

Behind our backs, but duly reported by Mother Mary, these holiday folk called us selfish, if not downright kiddist, for owning a place in such a prime position and equipping it solely for adults. They'd gasped at the lack of bunk beds and lectured us on discrimination. It was pointless to apprise them that, between us, Graeme and I have six children, and to try and explain that because the cottage is so small and the terrain so tough, it only made sense to target it at a specialised couples market. But I longed to tell these crusaders for children's rights that friends of ours further along the coast have a treehouse weekender available only to non-smoking, able-bodied, vegan gay couples.

The blooming jacarandas, soft and paintbox-purple, and the batty chorus of cicadas heralded the nearness of year's end and we began planning our first Bay Christmas. The water is at its most sparkling when the summer sun is blazing and we'd start each day with a dip at Putty Beach. Unused to such morning activity, I'd often fall asleep on the train into Central. I'd ring Graeme through the day and if he wasn't at home, I'd suspect he was in the surf and I'd sit at my desk in Surry Hills feeling hot and envious.

On Christmas Eve, I took an early train from the office back to the Bay and we had a quick dip before strolling down to the Coast Community Church on Araluen Drive. Graeme and I have always loved the fact that the two turn-off signs from Empire Bay Drive read: Hardys Bay RSL Club and, right below, as a sobering chaser, Community Church.

It is a small blue-grey wood and cement building, shaded by a lone palm looming like a votive candle. There's splendid irony in the fact it used to be the RSL Club before the present building was erected with its ranch-style verandah and low lines in a glade of tall trees on Heath Road. Carols by Candlelight was the lure on the night before Christmas, with a stage set up on the foreshore. Kids in pyjamas and pelicans by the pier, great gaggles of kookaburras in the trees chortling at us as we launched into 'Good King Wenceslaus' while we held our candles and song-sheets and the sun disappeared behind the headland, like a coin into a slot.

On Boxing Day, our very first tenants moved into Peacock Cottage with a fortnight's booking. As new and inexperienced landlords, we lay in bed over at Thistle Do holding our breath and waiting for things to go wrong.

'The kookaburras will be waking them up about now,' muttered Graeme, grabbing for the clock. It was four a.m. 'It rained overnight,' I reminded him. 'At least that means the brush turkeys won't be doing their tai chi exercises on the tin roof. It's too slippery.'

We dozed fitfully until six when the phone rang. 'Don't answer it!' he commanded. 'I bet they've had two showers in a row and the hot water's run out.'

'It's our wake-up call,' I grumbled. 'You booked one last night so you could get up and sneak over there and secretly hose Alfredo's droppings off the bonnet of their car.'

He said he didn't think he'd bother after all, what with the overnight rain. 'You didn't forget to tell them about the peacock, did you?' he accused. 'I left a detailed note,' I replied, 'inside the book on snakes next to the first-aid kit.'

He groaned and slapped his forehead in despair as he stumbled out of bed to find his binoculars for a quick search of the opposite shore for flashing ambulance lights.

'What if they hate fish?' he asked over breakfast, referring to Phil's piscean carpentry. 'No one hates fish, as such,' I replied. 'Some people are allergic to them but, you know, that's not the same as just being required to turn a fish tail to open the toilet door.'

'When Mother Mary told them about the house, do you think she mentioned the jigsaw? We should ring

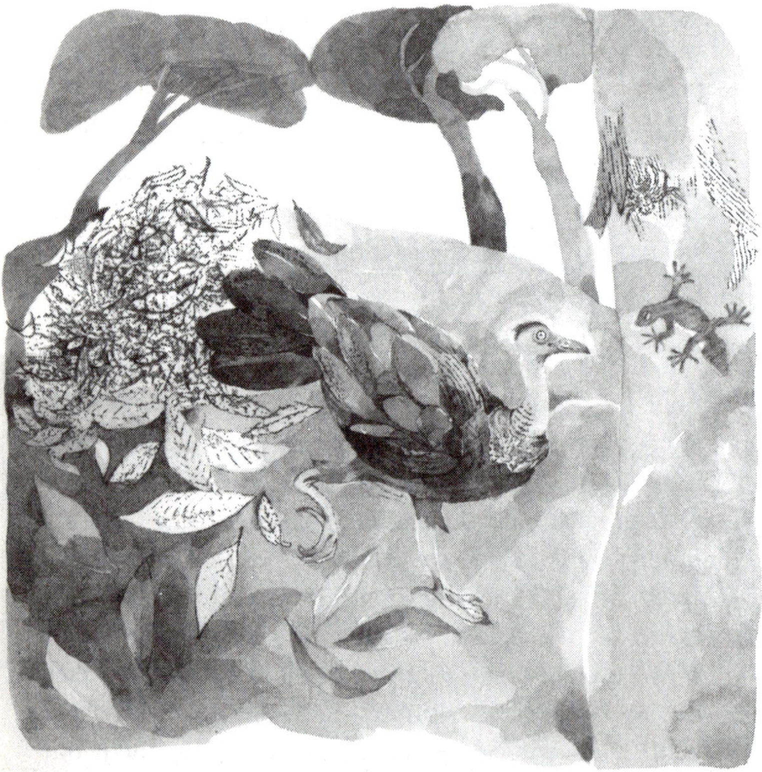

Brush Turkeys

At the Bay, wild turkey doesn't refer to a mellow drink. Big, black brush turkeys scrabble around the gardens giving instant truth to poet Ogden Nash's observation that 'there is nothing more perky than a masculine turkey'. They eat insects, native fruit and seed and can often be seen perched on the feeder trays that Bay folk fill with wild bird seed for galahs and lorikeets. Balanced on these bowls, often on the railings of a high deck, the brush turkeys look about as unlikely as pterodactyls. Expect to be visited by these Bay inhabitants if you are camping at Putty Beach Reserve; other resident wildlife includes the northern brown bandicoot, swamp and bush rats, sugar gliders, swamp wallabies and echidnas.

The male brush turkey builds an incubator mound for his mate's eggs, scratching up much of the leaf litter and mulch of Bay gardens in the process. Garry and Greg of Headlands, a hideaway retreat built high over Pretty Beach, have what they've dubbed a Turkey Tree, upon which seven of the birds roost, as still as shags. Headlands did have an organic vegetable garden and crops of bananas until the brush turkeys discovered the plots and demolished the lot.

and tell them a piece is missing...I told you it wasn't a good idea.'

'Oh, cut it out!' I yelled. 'The games and puzzles are only for show. You'd feel cheated if you rented a beach cottage and there wasn't a battered old box of Scrabble and a jigsaw of the Eiffel Tower. It doesn't mean you intend to do anything with them.'

'It's still raining,' Graeme muttered, although really he was thrilled about this unscheduled watering of his garden. 'I suppose they'll watch videos...I guess they must be cross about the weather.'

And so it continued. A fortnight of endless worrying that strangers who'd paid to stay in our 'charming Caribbean-style cottage filled with books' were finding it low on charm, high on mosquitoes, and the only Barbados connection they could discover was old videos of Australia vs West Indies Test matches.

As novice landlords, we worried about water pressure, mattress softness, the finer workings of washing machines and pop-up toasters, barbecue mechanisms and the table manners and early-morning etiquette of myriad birdlife. One night I watched an episode of television's lovable lard-mouths, the Two Fat Ladies, and heard Clarissa reveal she'd once shot a country neighbour's peacock, mistaking it for a rabbit. 'Then what?' asked Jennifer. Clarissa proceeded to describe how she'd cooked it and I lay awake all night imagining Alfredo as the roast of the day at Peacock Cottage.

What we loved about life by the Bay with its barefoot culture, disregard for clocks, spidery gardens and fish-and-chips cuisine may not have been everyone's cup of tea. So for two weeks we talked of little else. Graeme drove past Peacock Cottage six times a day and reported back to me. Surf towels were waving on the deck like so many victory flags. One night, he smelled sausages sizzling and heard loud laughter as Alfredo, who showed no sign of pining for me, the fickle scoundrel, spread his tail on the roof of their station-wagon like the lord of the manor swishing his splendid cloak.

Finally, Mother Mary confirmed that all went swimmingly, apart from a few minor emergencies: a repair to the VCR, a broken blender. 'I didn't let you know earlier,' she said, handing us a cheque, 'because I didn't want you two to worry about a thing.'

•

Phil was also one of our first renters. His two sons, Tim and Simon, down each school-holiday period from boarding college near Moree, came to love Peacock Cottage so much that we agreed Phil could have a six-month lease until our extensions were built. How naive we were bandying about a figure like six months. Little did we know of the labyrinthine workings of the many mysterious departments of Gosford City Council. 'They move with glacial majesty,' remarked a knowing neighbour.

As we cleaned the cottage and put in fresh fruit and flowers to welcome Phil and his lads, we realised there was no hot water. The old-fashioned hot-water tank was in the roof and some error in plumbing had occurred when we'd had the new vanity cabinet and bowl installed in the bathroom. On the phone to Mother Mary, who had an emergency plumber in the door and up a ladder in less than half-an-hour. We stood below listening to a stream of mumbled expletives. Finally, he poked his head out and asked us who'd done the plumbing. 'I don't remember his name,' said Graeme. We both knew how he'd been hired, however—he was a friend of Pe'er. To this day, we have nightmares about Peacock Cottage suddenly exploding under pressure, a victim of loose pipes and wrongly connected valves.

Phil came up the steps and I steered him onto the deck to admire the view and say hello to Alfredo. But through the window, Tim and Simon had spotted the plumber's legs dangling through the ceiling manhole and were in fits of giggles.

At the end of the holiday season, before Phil moved in for his six-month stay and after the Summer People, as we Bay 'old-timers' so smugly call them, had trickled away, we invited a series of close friends to try out Peacock Cottage and report back to us with brickbats and bouquets. There we were across at Thistle Do, feeling completely disconnected, only able to snatch the odd night in our 'real' home. We had no proper idea if the cottage was comfortable and summer renters gave little specific feedback—although one did complain to Kerrie at Mother Mary's of the appalling lack of an espresso machine.

Another renter had suggested we put in ceiling fans but we'd done all the necessary measurements and although Graeme and I are short, we'd have decapitated taller guests with the sweeping blades. As it was, Graeme knew that if his two most towering friends, actor Bruce Spence and playwright David Williamson, were to visit, they'd have to remain outside on the deck and be served cocktails through the ferry-boat windows.

Jane and Norman reported there wasn't enough shelf space in the bathroom to place two toiletries bags plus a hairdryer and suchlike. Phil leapt into action, carving fish supports at either end of a new wooden shelf. Hilary and Steve had no complaints. Hilary, like me, is a Piscean and there could never be too many fish in either of our lives. As they drove off, she shouted that she wanted Phil to come and see her McMahons Point apartment. Steve just looked resigned to the prospect of more fishy business. Catherine merely said everything looked so distressed. We think she was referring to Phil's fashionably peeling furniture rather than to us.

My toddler godson, Sebastian, arriving with his parents, Christine and Melvin, slept in the car all the way from Sydney but had been brimming with excitement about 'Susan's beach house' before they set out. Christine woke him as they arrived at Thistle Do, at low tide. He got out, looked at the mud, the ibis scratching around, the rowboats with their leprous paintwork flung about the flat, and a tear rolled down his cheek. 'Poor Susan didn't find a very beautiful beach,' was all he could manage and his depression didn't lift until I drove him up the hill and around to Putty Beach, where a Cornetto and a view of the surf cheered him up no end.

Sue and Andrew enjoyed themselves enough to stay an extra night but Andrew screwed up his nose at the bird droppings on the deck railing. We had visions of putting tiny little nappies on the kookaburras and rainbow lorikeets for the benefit of squeamish guests. They approved of the presence of Alfredo, the Bay boulevardier, however, and given the appropriateness of their names, took to renaming themselves Mr and Mrs Peacock for the duration of their stay.

Everyone agreed we needed glass doors on to the deck and Sue jokingly suggested an inclinator for an easier passage up the stone steps, Mayan-like in their slope and steepness, that Graeme was busily building. Maybe not such a flippant suggestion: we still talk of the need for an inclinator when our aged knees finally let us down. A few of the very high homes on Araluen Drive come with these outdoor elevators and they're made much of in real-estate advertisements, although sometimes a bobby-dazzler of a blooper appears. My 'Bay Watch' file has one ad for a house with 'four-person incinerator', another with 'tall French widows' and, best of all, a pole home with 'a huge, north-facing dick'.

All our visitors loved Graeme's garden. What had been a grassy rise from street level to the latticed area below the house was now terraced with rock walls and planted with citrus trees, palms, cycads, black boys, shell ginger, star jasmine, gloriosa lilies, birds-of-paradise, ornamental bananas, frangipani and hibiscus. On two brief holidays to Bali, he'd roamed resort estates, making notes, taking photos and talking to gardeners. Trundling about in his ute with that cap pulled ever lower over his head, he'd become a familiar figure at the two local nurseries. Orders were placed and promptly filled for such exotica as peach-coloured and white bougainvillea and traveller's palms 'like the ones Susan says are in front of Raffles Hotel in Singapore'. The nurserymen, forever wide-eyed at Susan's international botanical experiences, slipped extra plants and bulbs into Graeme's orders.

•

'The Garden of Adin Sonter' is the no-nonsense title of a section in *Good Old Woy Woy* by the late local historian Charles Swancott. Included is a picture of this successful nurseryman of the 1940s attending his ten-feet-high sweet peas. 'His floral garden was recognised as the largest in the southern hemisphere,' declared Swancott of Sonter's estate which included spreads of gladioli, daffodils, hyacinths, freesias and tuberose plus a dam planted with water lilies. Late in life, his health failing, Sonter sold his precious land to a construction company which promptly filled it with three and a half feet of sand dredged from Woy Woy Channel for a housing subdivision.

Its centrepiece slash was named Sonter Avenue, still there today, off Brick Wharf Road, the channel-side strand once tangled with wild roses and flannel flowers and home to mobs of wallabies. I wonder if it would be any consolation to Sonter to know that the streets radiating from his namesake have been dubbed, in a frenzy of alliteration, Camellia Crescent, Daffodil Drive, Azalea Avenue and Primrose Place.

•

Peacock Cottage's garden is Graeme's pride and joy and I think it was while he was digging and pruning and building stone walls and steps that he fell truly in love with the Bay.

The early days had been harder for him than for me. If I was at the office working along at my usual routine, he would often be alone at the Bay. In the city, he'd been able to duck out for coffees, to chat with friends, do the daily drop-in at his management agency, Shanahan's, and shop at his favourite stores—what I call 'Gucci groceries' from Mensa in Paddington, Fuel in Surry Hills and the upper-crust, lower-case jones the grocer. At the Bay, a stroll around nearby Woy Woy Supermarket or a chinwag with his new mates at an array of hardware stores was not quite the same. And when I was overseas, it became unbearable. He hated being alone at the Bay at night. It was isolated, lonely and prone to blackouts. We soon learned to have candles permanently on hand and got into a routine of saving documents on our computers every few minutes as the power would shut down with no warning.

He began to find reasons for us to stay more often in Surry Hills. But only for two nights at a time—the garden would lure him back, like a demanding mistress. In those months, I discovered the essential difference between us: I love being alone and he hates it. As an only child and a single parent, I've always been used to enormous degrees of space. Graeme has been married twice—we joke that I'm not his third wife, but his 'last' one—with two children from each marriage and he has always been in a relationship of some sort. My adjustment to the cut-off quality of the Bay was almost instant and any outside intellectual stimulation I needed could be found at the office or via daily phone calls with my dearest friend, Christine.

But while Graeme wrestled with an unaccustomed feeling of isolation, he also found himself the subject of envy. The series 'SeaChange' had started on ABC television and suddenly everyone wanted to do 'the Pearl Bay thing' and move somewhere less complicated and more optimistic. Like Sigrid Thornton's screen character Laura Gibson, they longed to throw in the serious city job and drop out at a quirky seaside settlement where no one wore ties or high heels or remembered to lock their front doors.

Interior design shops were quick to catch on to the trend, with book-cases made of old row-boats, mermaid motifs, shells and coloured starfish all appearing. Every guest at the Bay brought a house-warming item decorated with a striped bathing box or a sea creature. Lovely, apposite collectibles and as easy to find, apparently, as such countrified things as pot-pourri, bunches of dried flowers and old ginger jars had been the previous season.

'To do a Laura Gibson' became part of the office vernacular that summer and social commentators began writing columns and opinion pieces about the 'SeaChange phenomenon'. In the late 1990s, urban Australians, they opined, were looking not for cosmopolitan pleasures but for ordinariness. The ideal tonic was thought to be on offer at the sort of seaside place which came with a permanent air of holiday, relatively free from such now-common city plagues as drugs and violent robberies.

The popularity of the series was echoed by the success of 'Ballykissangel', 'Hamish Macbeth' and 'The Vicar of Dibley'. Plot points: take a fish out of water and place him or her in an alien pond populated by strange but lovable characters, stir and then allow to settle. 'SeaChange' is filmed at the fishing village of Barwon Heads in Victoria but Hardys Bay could have been the model as, geographic similarities aside, we, too, have a cast of characters worthy of a television soap—not to mention an actual soap star, Judy Nunn of

'Home and Away' fame, ensconced by the water with her husband, Bruce Venables, writing romantic novels on her non-acting days, calling out to Adam the Gardener not to mow the lawn so loudly.

Mother Mary would be our choice to play the female lead in any Hardys Bay pot-boiler—the doyenne of the Bay, on hand in any crisis, broad-shouldered and sexy and given to changing her hair-colour according to mood. On Melbourne Cup day, as we all gathered in the Old Killcare Store for a lunch turned on by the two Pauls—P1 and P2, as these refugees from the inner-city espresso beat became fondly known—it was Mother Mary who brought the house down during the post-race karaoke session. Crouched low over a microphone, hair flopping forward (jet black that week), she launched into her rendition of 'Fever' with all the coquetry of a torch singer.

Later that evening as we took a constitutional along Araluen Drive to try and walk off the effects of too much daytime champagne, the party at the Old Killcare Store was still in full swing. Gordon and John from the neighbouring general store were weaving across the road with champagne on silver trays and white starched napkins folded over their arms, like taller versions of the manic Manuel from 'Fawlty Towers'. Through the windows we glimpsed Postmistress Pat, usually so brisk and efficient behind the counter attending to stamps and padded post-bags. Slowly dancing, with arms stretched high, her curled hair bobbed to the beat as if faraway jungle drums were calling.

We have no Diver Dan, the handsome, laconic 'SeaChange' character played by David Wenham. But we do have Dylan and Joe, sons of Mother Mary, with their brooding Celtic looks and gleaming smiles. And handsome Adam, married to Ellen, Mother Mary's daughter.

Adam appears to organise his gardening commitments according to the position of the planets and how the surf is running. Melbourne columnist Lawrence Money tells me he has a theory about tradesmen and handymen and their inability to show up when agreed. You answer their ads which promise free quotes and insist there is no job too small, he says, and they sound absolutely normal and quite enthusiastic and you agree on a time and place. All mythical, it transpires. 'Are they professional pranksters who are wearing rubber noses and Groucho glasses when you speak to them on their mobiles?' he wonders.

'My growing suspicion is that there was no real mystery about the *Marie Celeste*,' Lawrence continues. 'It was actually a ship full of Melbourne tradesmen on a holiday cruise and the concentration of so many in one location caused spontaneous evaporation.'

Make that Melbourne tradesmen and Central Coast gardeners, Lawrence. When Adam did appear, it was often as if via a puff of smoke. Suddenly he'd turn up, ambling among the trees, and settle in for a chatty assessment of Graeme's gardening techniques. When there was rock-walling and digging to be done, he'd bring a team of local tradies who'd work at a cracking pace while Adam stared moodily into the middle distance as if hoping for a sign from God that the Putty Beach waves were up.

But Adam's advice and designs were first class and despite his airy disregard for clocks and timetables, the Hanging Gardens of Hardys Bay, as the locals had dubbed our once-lawned front yard, were assuming the intricate beauty of a Mughal emperor's pleasure patch. The soil on our southern side of Hardys Bay is dark, rich and wormy and Graeme found it was almost a matter of throwing in a seed and leaping back while it took root. Courtesy of a long wet spring and summer that first year, the tropical plantings ran riot. Travel author Jan Morris has written of Caribbean foliage 'purring with luxurious relief' after tropical storms, and our Bay trees and shrubs showed a similar contentment. The garden had become supple, full and fecund, the leaves spongy and fleshy, and the trees beneath the deck were clawing toward the railings like triffids.

•

But we were still living at Thistle Do, our lives put on hold while the Council queried in meticulous detail every point of Cedric's plans. We'd proposed a rear cliffside pavilion, to be joined to Peacock Cottage by enclosed steps. It was viewed with suspicion as a dual occupancy, even though each component was clearly too small to live in and the extension had no kitchen. Browsing through a file of papers left behind by the previous owners, we found plans for a proposed side-verandah extension that had been submitted to Gosford City Council in August 1955. As the work had never been done, we joked that the architect's drawings probably were still in a Council clerk's pending file.

Phil had moved in as our tenant and spent most of his days at nearby Woy Woy in a big workshop he'd rented. He was 'fished out' by this time and had decided to buy up and restore old wooden boats. We started to see them all over the Bay, for sale at the Marina, at anchor, chugging along, often with Tim or Simon at the tiller during holidays. Our favourite was painted bright red with a white canopy slung casually, like a draped scarf. It could have puttered its way out of a Walt Disney cartoon. Phil definitely had gone coastal.

Graeme's daughter Harriet was with us most weekends, sometimes with a school friend, and other guests came and went. If we all felt energetic, there'd be picnics at Lobster Beach. The walking trail meanders off between two houses in High View Road at Wagstaffe, around the Bay toward our peninsula's headland. It's a suburban entry point to what is a lovely bushland trail through gums, banksia and scrubby acacia. Although it's not flat and there are no proper boardwalks, it reminds me of the track through Noosa National Park on the Queensland Sunshine Coast. There's the same sense of stepping from suburbia into a wild and lovely place. In Noosa's case, Hastings Street, with its parade of chic shops and restaurants, all but merges into the national park where there are birds galore and koalas high in the trees, bundled in sleep. But the Lobster Beach trail's main form of wildlife is the mosquito, specifically the kamikaze variety intent on staging do-or-die missions on bare flesh.

The Lobster Beach trail is steep enough to require a few stops on the way and just when we'd reach the top of the rise, there were all those plank-edged steps down again to the beach, including a rough scramble to actually get to the sand. It could be a major undertaking with a laden Esky and picnic basket but the endeavour was always well rewarded by cellophane-clear water, a secluded cove and the possibility of snorkelling—unless, of course, we'd brought the snorkel but left the mask in the car, all those steps away. The easier access is by boat, which Graeme and I always intended to do when we organised the Zodiac rubber boat languishing somewhere in the bowels of Thistle Do's overflowing garage.

According to the local environment society, the Killcare Wagstaffe Trust, there's a group dedicated to clearing Lobster Beach of weeds and pests and regenerating native species. Lantana, bitou, privet, camphor laurel, milkweed and ochna are all in their sights. Putty Beach is the chosen turf of the Bitou Bush Bashers who've been toiling since the late 1970s to rid the region of this dreaded weed. Gosford City Council actually has a Tree Preservation Officer and a Bush Regeneration Officer and has poured money into a Coastal Management Study of beach systems and bluffs south of MacMasters Beach. When I discovered this, I managed to feel slightly better disposed toward the Council, but the plans for our extensions to Peacock Cottage were still languishing in a bureaucratic black hole.

Other guests did some exploring behind Peacock Cottage up into the ridges of Bouddi National Park. Because of the erosion that can be caused, horse riding is no longer permitted, with on-the-spot fines of several hundred dollars imposed by rangers. You'd need to be a mountain goat to attempt some of the Bouddi's steep trails but that didn't stop Graeme setting off in expeditionary style shortly after we bought the cottage. He actually got to the top of our ridge but, looking down, lost sight of any rooftops and became disoriented. He decided to walk along the dirt track in the general direction of Killcare until he found an easy slope to climb down. He wandered much further than he had imagined because when he finally came careering down, amid showers of falling stones, he was in a completely unknown backyard, an uninvited guest, emerging like a feral madman in the middle of a ladies afternoon tea. He was sent on his way with a strong cuppa and a set of directions.

Some of our regular guests just pottered about the Bay proper, loving its aspic-set quality. 'Fifties Australiana,' was how Jenny put it. She bought a plastic shark of gunmetal grey with a killer grin at a Woy Woy petrol station and put it on the rear-window shelf of her car. 'To scare off tailgaters on the F3,' she explained.

Sandy and Greg came to visit in their boat, tying up at the jetty outside Thistle Do and climbing our steps with trays of fresh oysters. All these city friends spoke about the 'small kindnesses' of the Coast, especially help with directions, even when locals scratched their heads and said, 'You'd be better off if you didn't start from here.' Rather like those stories of Irish country folk telling tourists to turn left at the third cow.

They told us about 'human' driveway service at petrol stations and shop assistants who carried groceries to cars. We didn't tell them that there was only so much kind advice one actually needed, especially when being woken at dawn by a passer-by hammering at the window of Thistle Do to let us know of a carpet snake coiled by our garbage bin.

Throughout the year, we designed various itineraries for visitors, discovering in the process that the Coast has much to offer beyond the obvious seaside distractions. The New South Wales National Park and Wildlife Service runs Discovery Tours, graded according to suggested fitness levels, which involve canoeing on Mooney Mooney Creek, nocturnal excursions with torches to spot fauna in the Brisbane Water National Park, coastal walks from Patonga to Ettalong, and family bushwalks, complete with buns and billy tea, through the Dharug

National Park to Baiame Creek, 'home of the lyrebird'. All the activities have a sound educational element, and some cost as little as a few dollars.

When issuing visitors with maps, we'd mark favourite lookouts—Staples on the Patonga Road, Marie Byles on the Scenic Road—and direct them to the Bulgandry Aboriginal Site, off the Woy Woy Road, with its fine sandstone carvings. The Gurringai tribe 'have left behind such a rich legacy of rock engravings, charcoal and ochre drawings and axe-grinding grooves', reads the New South Wales National Parks and Wildlife Service literature. Who needs Marree Man, we'd scoff, when we have Bulgandry Man.

CHAPTER FOUR
Pioneers and Property Developers

'You grabbed the axe and built yourself. It stopped undue dreaming and flashness...by the time you dug the well and the privy and made a road out, any over-enthusiasm had mellowed somewhat and you made quite a good neighbour.'

Vic Wamsley, as quoted by Charles Swancott in
Gosford and the Kendall Country

Hardys Bay doesn't appear on all maps of the New South Wales Central Coast; frequently the entire area is named as Killcare. When we first told Sydney friends we'd bought a weekender at Hardys Bay, some misheard it as Hervey Bay, on the Queensland coast north of Noosa. 'Oh, well,' said one, 'I guess you'll get used to the drive and at least you can watch the whales.'

What we'd liked most about the hidden inlet in our early days was that it's a destination in itself. Once you drive down the hill to the Bay, there's nowhere else to go. Turn left and you can motor on to Pretty Beach and Wagstaffe but you then have to double back on the same road out of 'town'.

Originally it was simply part of Ward's Bay, called after William Ward, the first settler at what became Killcare, a name apparently bestowed purely for its carefree connotations. In those days, apostrophes were allowed. When we moved into Thistle Do, I rang Australia Post to enquire about the lack of apostrophe in Hardys Bay. 'We have outlawed apostrophes,' I was told, with some crispness. I also asked about Wagstaff versus Wagstaffe as both spellings occur on road signs. 'Can't find any such place,' she said, flicking through the directory of postcodes.

The UBD directory of the Central Coast recognises Wagstaffe, tucked in behind Box Head, where Brisbane Water meets Broken Bay. The 'e' certainly was in evidence, whether or not as an ornamentation, when the Wagstaffe Point Estate was subdivided in 1906. Local historian Beryl Strom confirms that as far as contemporary usage goes, the Geographical Names Board has officially assigned the final 'e'. It may not rate suburb status, but Wagstaffe residents have the same postcode as Hardys Bay, Pretty Beach, Killcare, Empire Bay, Daleys Point, St. Huberts, Booker Bay, Umina and Ettalong. How snug, to be so little that Australia Post corrals you. People talk of dropping out to a 'one phone book town' but the entire Coast is contained in one directory, and that includes the Yellow Pages.

I had imagined that my research into the early days of the area would mean weeks, if not months, nose-deep in Lands Department records, newspaper files and reference books at Sydney's Mitchell Library. The process was made much easier through the discovery of a number of books of local history and legend by Charles Swancott, a stalwart of the Brisbane Water Historical Society. Mostly written in the 1960s, and billed by the author as 'history with humanity', the publications are jam-packed with detail and were well received in their day, enthusiastically reviewed by the Sydney press, with Swancott even being heralded as 'the Gibbon of Gosford', a prestigious comparison with Edward Gibbon, author of the monumental five-volume *History of the Decline and Fall of the Roman Empire*.

Swancott settled at Booker Bay in the 1920s, seduced by 'the peace of the place, the grassed streets, the charm of the beaches and waterways'. He's no longer alive but reading his works made me realise the importance of anecdotal history. He tells tales of, among many colourful others, Lobster Bill, Knocker Howard, John Peeling Ball and The Blackwall Miser. Of the redoubtable Ann Piper who gave birth to 24 children, all of whom survived, and who died just short of her one-hundredth birthday. And of the blind William Boston who ran the Punt Ferry at Erina Creek for more than 20 years. 'He made up by feeling what he missed in sight,' observed

Swancott. 'It was no use giving him a halfpenny and pretending it was a shilling, or a penny and stating that it was a florin.'

Swancott tends to be rather repetitive and occasionally contradictory in his writing but he spins a great yarn, sometimes involving himself, as in the case of his account of the Coastal version of 'Dad's Army' during World War II. Swancott joined the Volunteer Defence Corps but uniforms and weapons were in short supply. To repel a possible Japanese invasion of Pearl Beach or Ocean Beach at Umina, Swancott recounts that he and his fellow soldiers kept guard with dummy wooden rifles, a few beer bottles and 'whatever rocks we could find'.

Elaine Fry of the Brisbane Water Historical Society pointed me toward two historical monographs honouring the women of the Central Coast. Their stories may not bear the stamp of discovery or derring-do but their lives were remarkable for the hardships they endured and their small daily triumphs. Florence May, for example, was a notable mechanic and she and her husband, George, began a hire car business just before the outbreak of World War I. Her daughter, Edna Stone, recalled Florence's story of chasing a stolen vehicle through Ourimbah with the local policeman as her passenger. Despite the officer's urgings, she refused to go any faster than the official speed limit. Her eight-seater Nash was the second car to drive along the new road to Killcare; a small single-seater beat her by four hours to win a case of whisky.

Betty Eloise Kirk was rowed from Davistown to classes at Empire Bay School where her first teacher was Mr Tory; as was the custom at small schools, he would have taught everything, from scripture to sport. His wife instructed the girls in sewing and Wattle Day was always celebrated with the choosing of a Queen and Flower Girls and a performance of 'The Graceful Flowering Wattle'.

'Fish and crabs were plentiful with oysters on the rocks in abundance,' remembered Betty. 'Blackberries were picked for jam and pies.' Una Davis recalled Empire Bay School as the earlier Cockle Creek Public School; the name was changed in 1910. 'The children from Davistown had to cross a bay 400 yards wide by rowing boat,' according to Una, 'then walk a mile to reach the one-room school. There was a quarter-acre playground with a deep creek at the back which sometimes flooded. The classroom seated 25 pupils and on the porch were hooks to hang our wet weather gear and our hats and the boys spun their tops there.

'In the grounds marbles were played, there was a big swing and hurdy gurdy, also a cricket pitch and space for rounders. The drinking water came from a tank. The two toilets were built over a hole in the ground.'

Una also recounted that when it was too windy for the boat crossing, she stayed at home with her mother, and she loved those cosy days. But the education of girls was not a priority of the era and she'd be kept home most Fridays, in any weather, to polish the brass doorknobs and bed-ends and to whitewash the steps.

In the 1940s, Doreen Knowles attended Empire Bay School, still reached from Davistown by rowboat, with that mile to trudge from the bank. But on weekends, recreational rowing was all the go. 'We all knew how to row a boat, nearly every house in those days had a boat to go with it,' she recalled. From the age of about 16 onwards, she travelled around by ferry. 'On the moonlight excursions on the old *Southern Cross* there would be someone playing a piano on board and we would all have a sing-song... The ferries created a wonderful atmosphere which Cockle Creek lost when they stopped running.'

Minard Fannie Crommelin's first positions were as 'housemaid and telegraph messenger' but she was to become Woy Woy's first postmistress in 1906. Margaret Forrester of the Brisbane Water Historical Society has researched Minard's life and discovered that she was not accommodated in 'the four-room weatherboard cottage suitably fitted up for a post office' she'd been promised but directed to 'a shack of corrugated iron partitioned off to make three rooms, and a "lean-to" at the side' where she discovered 'the entire material for the new post office was contained in a quarter-sized fruit case'.

Undaunted, Crommelin spent five years working hard at Woy Woy and developing an interest in local flora. Years later, after extensive travel around Australia and overseas, she purchased seven acres at Pearl Beach, adjoining a reserve, and had built one large cottage and two small cabins where naturalists could stay and study coastal flora and fauna. She succeeded in having the 950-acre reserve between Pearl Beach and Patonga gazetted as a sanctuary in 1941 and the Crommelin Biological Research Station at Pearl Beach stands in her honour.

Laura Alice Pickett was postmistress at Avoca Beach during World War II: 'We had seven subscribers... and we only had one line to Gosford. The worst feature was getting a trunkline call through because we had a coast-watching station at Cape Three Points near the Captain Cook Memorial at Copacabana... Every plane and ship that went by had to be reported... So of course you'd be on a trunk call and all of a sudden "bang" they'd want the line and you had to get off.'

Ruby Dora Hicks, also late of Avoca, remembered a big bushfire and all the neighbours rallying to fight it. She went to make them some tea and 'there was a snake and a goanna in my kitchen and a frog on the telephone'.

•

'After passing a bar that had only water for small vessels, entered a very extensive branch from which the ebb tide came out so strong that the boats could not row against it in the stream; and here was deep water...Pelicans and a variety of birds were seen here in great numbers.'

Letter from Governor Phillip
to Lord Sydney, May 15, 1788

Governor Phillip had explored what was dubbed 'the North-East Arm of Broken Bay' in 1788 and 1789, just five weeks after the arrival of the First Fleet. In 1825, it was renamed Brisbane Water to honour Sir Thomas Brisbane, then Governor of New South Wales. The region boasted valuable resources of timber, essential for boat-building, but overland access from Sydney was difficult and no non-Aboriginal settlement had taken place until 1823, with James Webb generally regarded as Brisbane Water's first white land-owner. A census conducted in March, 1829, showed 15 householders, seven horses and 916 cattle. Ten years later, 315 persons were counted, including male and female convicts. By that stage, shingles for Sydney roofs were being cut in huge supply.

Shipbuilders, attracted by the plentiful supply of timber such as blackbutt, ironbark and white mahogany, formed settlements at Blackwall, Kincumber, Davistown and Terrigal. By 1844, a punt was in operation at Peats Ferry—named for pioneer George Peat—between Kangaroo Point and Mooney Point. When the first railway bridge was built over the Hawkesbury River in 1889, officially connecting city and coast, villages such as Gosford and Woy Woy rapidly expanded and other villages were founded around Brisbane Water. A road bridge was not built until 1945.

'Uncommonly desirable farms for small settlers' was typical of Government parlance of the day. The first settler at the Bay, in its southern corner, was James Mallen, or Mullen, depending on which records are consulted; the 1829 Census revealed he had '50 acres, 10 cleared and cultivated, and 26 horned cattle'. Like other farmers of the day, he would have cut logs and shingles and gathered shells to be sold for the manufacture of lime. A Land Determinations Map reproduced in Coastwatch's 'Bouddi Peninsula Study' shows Mallen's grant covered the stretch of land now occupied by Peacock Cottage.

It's not clear when Robert Hardy and his wife, Mary, came to live on Mallen's holding but it is known that they were in residence by 1891 and had started a vineyard in the vicinity of today's RSL and Citizens Club. Hardy made his own wine from a bitter brown grape and sold it by the gallon. Residents of Booker Bay used to arrive by boat at Hardy's plot, buy his plonk, picnic under his trees and then row home. This went on until about 1908, according to Swancott. It's a tradition still honoured under the Yum Yum tree, although we've not seen anyone actually row off from the dusk drinking sessions.

'Hardy was hard by name and nature,' wrote Swancott. 'He kept a pet black snake in the vineyard to guard against thieves... He kept an old shotgun always loaded with a few slugs for use on the birds which attacked the grapes. They were mostly honey eaters, finches and silver eyes. Hardy said that it cost him a bit for the powder and the shot, but "he could always eat the birds".

'He was a tough North Country man, canny and mean to a degree. He had a mole at the end of his nose which fascinated children... Though he grew grapes, he would not sell a pound of them but made wine of the lot. He had a wharf about 200 feet in length in front of his property; the decking was made from timber collected piece by piece from broken packing cases left on the wharves by steamers.

'Mr and Mrs Hardy invariably rowed over every Saturday afternoon to Booker Bay to visit Mr and Mrs Bogan, where they stayed for tea. He rowed so leisurely that if the tide was against him, his boat seemed to be anchored. When leaving the Bogans, Hardy would rub his hands together and say to his wife, "Well, lass, that's eighteen pence saved".'

Mrs Bogan became famous for a remark of her own. When asked by another visitor if she had a corkscrew to open a bottle of wine, it's said she replied, 'You'll find more corkscrews than prayerbooks in this house.' Apparently she was a practical woman, and resourceful with it. When she wanted two dozen eggs sent across to Booker Bay from Mrs Riley's poultry farm at Rileys Bay, she flew a pillow case from a tall sapling and upon seeing the makeshift flag flapping, one of the Riley boys would row over, carefully cradling the order.

Meanwhile, on the northern shores of Hardys Bay, where Thistle Do and the Killcare Extension Wharf now stand, William Ward's selection was swarming with wild bees attracted to the scented eucalypts. He went into the honey-producing business, as did other settlers. 'When they sighted a vessel out on the ocean,' wrote

Swancott, 'they took their honey down the hills to the beach, and rowed it in their whaleboats out through the Heads for sale to the seamen.'

It's unclear when Ward's Bay became Hardys Bay and indeed if it was named for Robert or for his descendants who continued to farm the area. William (the beekeeper) is commemorated by Wards Hill Road, the steep and accident-prone access road to the Bay and beyond from Empire Bay. Just around from the Bay proper, Pretty Beach originally was called Kourong Gourong; the first settler was William Spears who purchased 50 acres on February 7, 1835 for the fine sum of 12 pounds, 10 shillings. He built a hotel, The Sign of the Crooked Billet, and was Brisbane Water's first licensee of 'a Common Inn, Ale House or Victualling House', recognised to sell 'ale and other malt liquors and wine, cider, ginger beer, spruce ales, brandy, rum and other fermented or spirituous liquors'.

'The inn was built before the road was aligned and customers had to step down a foot to the bar floor. It was a port of call for the sailing ships' crews,' wrote Swancott, 'whenever they had the "excuse" of head winds beating up to Woy Woy, or of waiting for the ebb tide to go over the Half Tide Rocks.'

Later, according to Swancott's research, the inn became less popular, probably because of the advance of the railway and Pretty Beach's considerable distance from any station. It seems to have been supplanted by the Windbound Hotel and then Manly House; the latter had 22 guestrooms and a dance hall in its heyday but burned down in 1939.

Around from Pretty Beach, on the peninsula's next point, Patrick Mulhall settled on 50 acres in the 1830s. He dubbed his farm, which adjoined Crown Reserve land, Mount Pleasant and for a time the area was known as Mulhall's Point. According to the 1841 Census, Mulhall and his family lived in a timber house, ran 35 head of cattle, and had cleared 14 acres of land, of which seven were planted and farmed. Today, this is Wagstaffe Point, once famous for its cultivation of watermelons. Wagstaffe Point Estate was subdivided and presented for sale on December 22, 1906, advertised as 'the Manly of Brisbane Water' and 'undeniably the pick of the District'. Unbelievably, if you bought a block without a water frontage, you got a smaller one free, with wharf access for a boat. When further subdivisions were made between 1906 and 1920 from Wagstaffe to Killcare Extension, the 'estate' of Hardys Bay officially made the map.

Until 1902, public bathing during daylight hours had been banned. According to an early handbook of the Surf Life Saving Association of Australia, 'Thanks to the efforts of a small band of enthusiasts who defied the regulations, the restrictions were waived and bathing on the beaches became general. Thus was created a new field of pleasure in which the young and old of both sexes were enabled to enjoy together the combined benefits of the sun, sand and salt water with the utmost freedom.'

As the 20th century got into its stride and the puritanical Victorian era receded, there was a new pursuit of recreation and with that came the quest for sea-fresh air. At Booker Bay, Patrick and Sarah Murray ran the Retreat, a 'high class boarding establishment' where 'all modern conveniences' were offered. An advertisement of 1910 boasted that 'Sydney steamers call at our Wharf three times weekly'.

Old Gosford and District Album, a mostly pictorial book compiled by Gwen Dundon, contains a chapter on early weekenders at Hardys Bay. The first one was built of weatherboard in 1911 by William Montgomery of Belmore, Sydney, who called it So Long Letty. Between 1914 and 1926, he built a further three, Monterey, Sally, and You and I, all of fibro and named, Dundon suggests, for popular songs of the day.

Materials would have been brought in by boat; other weekenders of the era were known as Arizona, Cozy Corner and Mascotte. There was also a Turo, named for Turo Downes, an Aboriginal resident and former ship's mate who acted as the Bay factotum, keeping an eye on vacant cottages, doing odd jobs and taking parties to view the wreck of the *Maitland*, a ship which sank at what is now Maitland Bay in 1898. Turo had a reputation as a marvellous swimmer, according to Swancott. 'I recall seeing him plunge into the ocean from the rocks at Killcare Beach, swim into the sea caves and reappear with a threshing lobster.'

Another photo in Dundon's fine assembly shows the Victoria ferry boat conveying schoolchildren on an outing from Woy Woy to Hardys Bay. It was taken during World War I and all the ferry windows are wide open, with clusters of kids on the bow and several heads poked through each of the life-buoys as if they were portholes. In the background, where Araluen Drive hugs the shore today, is an enormous sign, as remarkable as the Hollywood lettering looming over Los Angeles, announcing Killcare. It had been constructed to announce the subdivisions of Killcare Estate in 1916.

The Patonga Estate, just around from today's chic settlement at Pearl Beach, was subdivided into 50 lots and sold in 1918. By 1925, there were 70 houses, many used as holiday shacks by Sydneysiders who travelled to Brooklyn by train and caught a ferry across. In his booklet of local folklore and history, *Patonga and Some of Its People*, Ben Smith has reproduced an advertisement designed to woo holidaymakers of that era. Using Cowan Creek in the Kuring-gai Chase as a base, the full-page announcement exhorted families to rent houseboats equipped with not just the essentials but the luxury of on-board pianos. 'It will add years to your life to spend a few weeks each year under its exotic influences,' promised Fairyland Boatshed of its Hawkesbury River surrounds. 'Just fancy how nice it is to catch a bucket of Nice Fresh Fish for breakfast!'

Further up the coast, John Moore had settled in Avoca in 1830, naming his selection for the Avoca River in County Wicklow—where 'Ballykissangel' is filmed today. He grew grapes for wine and did well with a plantation of dates. Today, this is one of the prime holiday havens of the Coast, its population swelling sixfold during the long summer break.

The Dunleith Guest House opened at North Entrance in 1895 and there were four guesthouses at The Entrance by 1912, the largest of which was the Bayview, with accommodation for 150 and 'comfortably furnished tents for those who prefer outdoor sleeping'. Apparently tents were a favoured way for many guesthouses to cope with the overflow at peak holiday times. In 1923, Lakeside was opened by Renee Johnson, who before marriage had been one of the Taylors, the family which owned The Entrance's four guesthouses. Renee advertised her property as 'the most up-to-date', inviting guests to enjoy 'the comforts of a refined home', with no mention of tents.

The holiday house boom came at the end of World War I. Beryl Strom suggests that's when the carefree names such as Avarest and Weona were given to 'weekenders'. 'A block of land and a fibro cottage,' she observes, 'preferably at the seaside, was considered "the ultimate".' The subdivision of The Entrance in 1920 led to 200 allotments being sold at the first auction and, when the Scenic Road was constructed between Kincumber and MacMasters Beach in 1926, subdivision of the latter soon followed. In her booklet *MacMasters Beach—A History*, Strom has reproduced a 1920s advertisement for Tudibaring Ocean Beach Estate, a subdivision of 113 allotments, the first at MacMasters Beach named for the MacMaster family from Scotland who settled there in 1838. Amid the adjectives and boasts of 'motor bus service' is a sketch of a woman in a wind-tossed dress on the edge of a hill, one hand holding a tree, the other waving out to sea, her hair flowing freely, the very epitome of seaside insouciance.

Woy Woy was rapidly expanding through that period, too, its place on the Great Northern Railway assuring its popularity. In September 1897, the *Gosford Times* reported that 'upwards of 9000 pleasure-seekers visited Woy Woy and Blackwall during last holiday season'. A figure of 400 persons a day was quoted, a significant number for the time. Boarding houses started mushrooming within proximity of the station and the waterways and in 1912, a subdivision called Cox's Estate was opened, making available hundreds of lots.

The *Woy Woy Herald* of the 1920s was well-stocked with advertisements placed by local businesses. Joan Fenton and Maureen McMahon, in their historical booklet published in 1997 for the centenary of the Woy Woy Hotel, point out the following services and wares: Mrs Gilan had an 'up-to-date' soda fountain and her scones were 'famous', the meat from Mr Evans the butcher was 'clean', Mr Bull advertised pedigree Jerseys ('good milkers') for sale and the intriguingly named American Misfit Parlour dealt in blouses, bodices and knickers.

Most creative and poetic of the advertisers was one C.N. Shakespeare of Blackwall who described his carrying business thus: 'Shakespeare of old was known as the Immortal Bard. But in C.N. Shakespeare's Carrying Business, no mortal thing is barred.' Graeme and I wondered if descendants of Mr Shakespeare could be in charge of writing the pun-infested sayings on the noticeboard at Ettalong Baptist Church.

'A saturnalia of drunkenness and dissoluteness' was one view of the fast-growing town expressed to the *Woy Woy Herald* on October 26, 1923, but potential residents and holidaymakers were not put off in the slightest and by 1927 the permanent population was 3500.

Apace with Brisbane Water resident numbers was the growth of holiday houses and fishing shacks. One recorded estimate suggests 10,000 weekenders by 1976 in the Gosford–Wyong shires. But thanks to the formation of the Bouddi Natural Park, as it was then known, in the 1930s, the coast between MacMasters Beach and Killcare, including the blue bowl of Hardys Bay, has remained largely undeveloped and zoning regulations ensure no high-rises or traffic lights.

•

The names of the Central Coast are a cross-stitch of Aboriginal terms and the legacy of the first settlers. The

pioneers and property developers

Surveyor General Sir Thomas Mitchell had decreed 'native names of places are to be in all cases inserted where they can be ascertained' but as Brisbane Water was opened up for development and subdivisions occurred, a host of names crept in, and some of the originals were discarded. One unfortunate casualty was Kourong Gourong, meaning 'fast sea', which became the self-important Pretty Beach, but at least the point before Half Tide Rocks still bears the name. Tudibaring gave way to MacMasters Beach, named for the first settler family, but the Aboriginal name still applies to the northern headland. The mellifluous Kangy Angy and Tumbi Umbi plus Patonga, named by Aborigines for its oysters, and Bouddi, thought to mean 'water breaking over rocks', still stand proud.

The locals love taking liberties with names. Woy Woy (which means, so perfectly, big lagoon) is often known as The Woy, Yow Yow or Why Why, Kincumber becomes Cucumber, and given the number of celebrities who holiday at Hardys Bay, I've renamed it Hardywood. There's a zany sense of geographic appropriation, too—Halekulani, Wyoming, Copacabana, Toronto and Niagara Park all get a look in, although there's not a hula-dancing troupe, cowboy ranch, sugar-loaf mountain, Canadian mountie or world-scale waterfall to be found. One of these bizarre connections started with Frederick Augustus Hely, who was the Principal Superintendent of Convicts when he acquired his acreage in 1824 and named it Wyoming.

Hely experimented with many crops around Brisbane Water at a time when early settlers were unsure just what was likely to flourish. He had citrus fruits, tobacco, maize, potatoes, wheat and vines under cultivation; the district was beginning to be known as 'Sydney's food basket'. Later, at Palmers Wharf near Bensville, Angus Beattie, son of the pioneer shipbuilder Edward George Beattie, bred Black Orpington fowls and Indian game and organised the district's first milk deliveries. Onions were also an important crop, and an 'orangery' was described at Wyoming in 1855.

In the late-1880s, with the advent of the railway, citrus-growing began on a commercial scale, with John Bourke of Davistown, a grower of prize Valencias, acknowledged as the pioneer of the Coast's orchard industry. These days, there's a thriving macadamia plantation in the Yarramalong Valley west of Wyong, ostriches are farmed at Wyee, local honey and limes are for sale at roadside stalls and exotic bulbs are sold at a Kulnura estate. Citrus wine is made at Holgate and the Central Coast is close enough to the Hunter Valley to be known as this leading vine-growing region's front door. Robert Hardy, who was an unknowing pioneer of the Coast's wine industry, would no doubt have approved.

CHAPTER FIVE
Green Peace

*And, softer than slumber, and sweeter than singing,
The notes of the bell-birds are running and ringing.*

from 'Bell-Birds' by Henry Kendall

Graeme swiftly renamed our plot of paradise the Mosquito Coast. Squadrons of the pesky little blighters dive-bombed his flesh each evening as he watered the gardens of Peacock Cottage. The terraces, lush and serried, had become operatic in scale, brocaded with brightly coloured flowers, from busy lizzies to bushes of lavender, wantonly spreading. The scorch of magenta bougainvillea, stockades of white-budded tuberose, tall and thin like ballerinas. The sort of garden that comes with hidden stands of bamboo, spiky succulents and the possibility of parrots.

A small aloe vera plant that had looked healthy enough when we bought the cottage was now the size of a rosette-worthy cabbage. Every time I passed it, I'd snap off one of its squashy tendrils so I'd have gel on hand to rub on Graeme's mossie bites.

He had become full of Bay intelligence about mosquito repellent measures. Apart from the obvious—mossie coils, citronella candles, zappers, fine nets suspended over beds and Rid roll-on or spray—he decided to invest in bush gear from an army disposal store. The mossies, who know a city slicker when they bite one, had been stinging clear through his Calvin Clone T-shirts from the Hong Kong markets and feasting on his bare arms as if presented with a juicy buffet.

So the gardening gear was upgraded to full battle fatigue. Most days he was dressed for a walk-on part in *Apocalypse Now* and all he lacked was a pith helmet with a beekeeper's veil hanging soft and gauzy, like a theatre-prop scrim. Meanwhile, on the occasions when I was allowed to help in the garden, mostly as hosing assistant, always under instructions, I was as bare-armed and carefree as a wood nymph.

In India, in the early 1980s, I had malaria and my blood has lacked any appeal for mosquitoes ever since. In a hospital at Mysore, in the south of India, I was installed in a private ward kept aside for the local maharajah and other princely personages. But such regal purdah did not guarantee better standards of hygiene. The day I saw the nurses washing needles in well water, I checked myself out and commandeered a government car to drive me to the airport in Bangalore. Eventually, shivering and hallucinating, I made it back to Sydney where my blood samples became a source of great interest among students of tropical medicine at Sydney University.

Aside from a few shuddering relapses, the malaria seems to be under control and I am no source of interest whatsoever for the mossies of the Bay. They land on my skin, twitch in disgust and fly away in search of richer pastures, usually found aboard Peacock Cottage's star gardener.

Then there were the Bay spiders, spinning as relentlessly as basket-weavers in heritage villages. Our big, burly trees were decorated with gauzy frills. The decks and window surrounds at Peacock Cottage were constantly festooned with webs. One afternoon Alfredo, usually fastidious about where he stepped, walked through a particularly large web and screeched at me until I gently removed all trace of what looked like a gossamer hairnet from his head.

Despite the suburban setting, we were living with near-pristine wilderness on our doorstep. I decided we had to hone our green credentials and be more particular about recycling. Mother Mary had already told us one of our neighbours collected cans to sell to a recycling depot on the Coast and he would often write little notes to the residents asking them to put their empty aluminium cans at the top of the Council recycling bin. Then he could creep out, like a phantom ninja in the night, and whisk the cans away for his recycling run before the Council garbage trucks made their early-morning pick-up. We never received one of his missives but we approved of his resourcefulness and stealth.

Graeme started a compost heap while Justin and I were holidaying on the Gold Coast's South Stradbroke Island. We stayed at Couran Cove, a newish eco-resort run by Justin's former boss, Alastair McCracken. Alastair has gone quite batty about self-composting toilets and worm farms and all manner of eco-centric practices. He's installed a Green Channel on the resort's in-house television system and guests can call up the electricity and water usage for their room and compare it to the desired total. There are rewards for good guests and mock penalties for bad.

I regaled Graeme with all this upon our return and it stole the thunder from his compost heap, which seemed to consist mostly of lemon skins from his vodka and tonics and mouldy teabags turning into small scientific experiments. We wondered how Peacock Cottage guests would react if we installed a monitoring system of their various usages. Those who'd rented via Mother Mary's office had all been model tenants but several did leave behind evidence of oddness. One Sunday evening, when we walked across from Thistle Do to clean up after a departed tenant and put out the garbage bins, we were greeted with several dozen empty bottles that once had contained pre-mixed Midori melon liqueur and lemonade. They were infested with ants, by now quite giddy from slurping up the green dregs. On top of the garbage was a torn nightgown, white and diaphanous.

We had visions of what must have been a melon-induced saturnalia on the deck. Something in the order of Botticelli's 'Primavera', with Alfredo guarding the coloured drinks, the swirls in his tail providing a complementary shade of crème de menthe.

With Graeme's compost heap in action, I felt duty-bound to make sense of recycling. Actually separating glass, plastic, aluminium and paper was no big deal but small questions kept arising. Does one take the lids off bottles and jars before the containers go in their dedicated bin? If so, where should the lids be put? Perhaps one should start a dedicated lid bucket in the hope Tonia Todman or another of those nifty television arty-crafty people presents a mesmerising segment on the art of making ersatz African tribal necklaces from gherkin jar tops.

I had hoped our move to the Bay would render me a more useful person: someone who could bottle preserves and become famous for her cross-stitch and produce award-winning cabbages. But with Graeme being such an ace gardener and cook, any latent skills of mine had little chance of an airing. I did take up watercolour painting, however, and sauntered around with my camera looking for artistic shots. I adopted a faux-feral wardrobe, rarely changing out of loose cargo shorts, old shirts and a Huckleberry Finn straw hat. 'Hardys Bay Nought Couture' we dubbed the look.

But one area where I can outshine Graeme is in the art of deciphering instruction manuals. It is a handy facility when buying furniture from that certain chain store with a name that rhymes with diarrhoea. One thinks a shelving unit has been paid for but what awaits at the delivery dock is a flat box, an allen key and a how-to brochure written by someone with English as, at best, a third language.

To say Graeme and I ended up spitting tacks during self-assembly exercises would be literal indeed but eventually we managed to construct several units, only one of which needed a phone book to even up its legs. On my list of New Year's resolutions for our first January at the Bay was the promise that I would learn the Swedish words for top, bottom, left, right and anti-clockwise.

•

It's said that going troppo means having gin for breakfast and forgetting the names of your children. Although we were relaxed in a way we'd never experienced while living in the city, things were far too busy for tropical torpor to take hold.

While Graeme's exertions in Peacock Cottage's ever more populated and fertile garden rendered him tanned and fit, I spent weekends at Thistle Do glued to a keyboard churning out columns and travel pieces. I did a long beach walk on Saturday afternoons, but it began to seem senseless to be living in such a watery paradise and not make the most of it.

We had regularly raced into the surf at Putty Beach during our first months of visiting the Bay on weekends but now it was time to explore the hidden coves of the Bouddi. One such hideaway spot we discovered is Little Beach, reached from the Scenic Drive between Maitland Bay and MacMasters Beach. It is a 10-minute walk from the carpark, along a fairly level track bordered with haughty kangaroo paws and towering rainforest trees, like the dense vegetation of a Rousseau painting, the sort that could swallow you up in one great green gulp. The undergrowth, too, is ferny and secretive—Henry Kendall's 'flowerful fairy lands'—and bell-birds call to each other through the cool shady air.

Closer to our Bay, Putty Beach Reserve lies off Putty Beach Drive, a turn down from the Scenic Drive, reached via a track bordered with wild lilies, wood irises, tea tree, banksia and wattle. During summer, the campsites are chock-a-block, the smell of sizzling sausages and onions hanging in the air. It's an idyllic spot if one is good at camping; there are 10 sites which have to be booked in advance and there's fresh water and firewood. The campsites at Little Beach and Tallow Beach are more primitive, but all are in the most idyllic of settings, with the bonus of abundant birdlife and good, but unpatrolled, beaches.

These reserves are part of the Bouddi National Park on the north entrance to Broken Bay, a protected area which was pioneered as a park by Marie Byles, a keen member of the Federation of Bushwalking Clubs, who explored the area in the 1920s. Her first expedition was in 1922, with three girlfriends in tow. 'One of them was Ester Waite,' wrote Byles of her adventure. 'She wore breeks, a garment no girl ever wore in those days, with a gigantic Colt automatic pistol at her hip. We slept on the beach...and we had a small difference next day on the best way through the very rough country between Bouddi and Kincumber. Two of the party went off on their own...a severe thunderstorm came up that afternoon. These two found a hospitable farmhouse near Kincumber, with comfortable beds, but Ester and I, despite our maps and compass, had to doss in a smelly cowshed.'

The Bouddi was administered by trustees until 1967 when the National Parks and Wildlife Service was set up and it became Bouddi State Park; the area was bestowed with full National Park status in 1975. It covers 1150 hectares of wooded hinterland, occasional rainforest and coastal heathland, and a special feature is its 'marine extension' of just over 287 hectares between Gerrin Point and Third Point; fishing is prohibited therein and it's well patrolled by park rangers.

Graeme and I decided we should camp out one night, a sort of rite of passage toward fully fledged Coastie status. We booked a site at the Putty Beach Reserve, paid the licence fee and borrowed the camping gear. That was the easy part.

We soon learned that one needs to be enormously coordinated to be a happy camper. All that unfolding of unwieldy amounts of canvas and positioning of pegs and blowing up of air mattresses and working out which end of the sleeping bag you should put your head in. I'd told Graeme I'd camped before but hadn't apprised him of the details. 'Did you meet any bears?' he enquired casually, as he sprayed every surface of the tent with insecticide, including the cheese and biscuits I'd put out for the cocktail hour.

'No bears, as such,' I replied, 'but there were some rumbling semi-trailers.' I told him how young Susan had camped on the grassed median strip of a motorway. The First Dorking Brownies (otherwise known as the Dorks; imagine what they called our sisters from Horsham) had become lost in blanket-like fog while on a bivouac so we made camp on a likely-looking verge which turned out to be bang in the middle of the motorway. But much to the delight of Susan, who had not been paying attention during the briefing on disposal of one's personal waste in the woods, our campsite was nice and close to a petrol station with adjoining toilet facilities.

Next time I camped it was in the Okavango Delta of Botswana—not with the Dorks, however, as the most exotic trip we ever made was a bird-watching sortie to Wimbledon Common. In Botswana, a rogue hippo, searching for his mate, mistook the grey bulk of the tent occupied by Christine and myself for his lost love. Becoming very excited at finding 'her' so still and ready, he began to amorously hump the canvas. Until the tent collapsed. Christine and I were eventually rescued by game rangers as we lay under our camp stretchers tying Girl Guide knots into our hankies and crying for our mothers.

In the Royal Chitwan National Park in Nepal, another adventuress friend, Jill, and I were camping in friendly fashion (the two-person tent had been stitched with Pygmies in mind) while on a tiger-spotting safari. I had already caused a small international incident by killing my hot-water bottle. Grabbing a stick and whirling about like a dervish, I had belted the daylights out of my stretcher thinking a snake had curled itself into a tight ball beneath the covers. The cookboy finally calmed me down enough to explain it was a 'hottie' he'd put there while Jill and I were having dinner by the campfire.

The meal turned out to have devastating effects upon the digestive systems of the two memsahibs, who tossed and turned upon their canvas cots like bloated blimps and took turns to scurry off behind bushes, lacking the muscular control required to make it to the faraway toilet block. Modesty was thrown to the winds. Literally.

Next morning, Jill informed me that at exactly 3.15 a.m. I had made the biggest, loudest and altogether most thunderous noise she had ever heard. 'Come off it!' I retorted. 'That was you!'

As we argued over who had been responsible for the almighty explosion, the cookboy arrived with breakfast ('Goodie, curried eggs!' said Jill) and settled our argument. 'I am telling you it was a tiger,' he reported. 'Just outside your tent. Let me show you the tracks.'

It was at that moment I gave up camping. In fact, as it was the beginning of the Chinese zodiac's Year of the Tiger, I informed Jill I'd be staying indoors for twelve months.

Graeme listened wide-eyed to my tales as we scraped the top layers off the cubes of cheese and had a small difference over who was meant to have packed the corkscrew. Let me just conclude that it was the longest night we've yet spent at the Bay—but I did drive home to fetch the corkscrew so we could open a bottle of wine and toast Marie Byles, who was made of much sterner stuff than either of us.

•

We'd been living at the Bay for about three months when I saw a sign outside the Woy Woy Public Pool advertising aquarobics classes three times a week. I'd just had stomach surgery at Sydney's Royal Women's Hospital and the thought of some gentle exercise in scissoring Esther Williams fashion was enormously appealing.

The water in the public pool was soft and warm, almost silky to the touch. The sort of faintly cloudy liquid my mother would have identified, in a flash, as a veritable soup of low-class diseases. The colour was pale green, like unripe lemons. 'Eau-de-Nil' we called it in my youth, when matched pastel accessories were quite the thing. But when I first saw the Nile, at the age of 30, it was the colour of liquid butterscotch and not at all like the coolness of my mother's best court shoes.

The green came not from the chlorine or the tiles but the reflection of the shed's roof—a great sweep of lime fibreglass dotted with dark patches of leaves fallen from overhanging trees. What with the filtered sun, the green canopy and the fluorescent lights, my skin took on a liverish hue.

I was early for the first lesson and could observe the arrival of my fellow exercisers, all chatty and chummy, decked out in giant cossies with torpedo bras and rubber bathing caps. I realised immediately it was a water-based version of a morning coffee circle; one woman even had photos of her grandchildren sealed in little plastic envelopes so they could be passed around safely by our wet hands.

Someone passed me a bathing cap, but I declined with a smile. Impossible to explain how it feels being let loose with free-flowing hair and a two-piece at a common Council pool. I was banned from such germ-ridden dens when I was a child. That was the era of bugs, not drugs. Long before the fear of funny cigarettes being passed around behind the toilet block, the possible transfer of mumps, measles and meningitis kept my mother sick with worry. Not to mention what words I might learn and how my already fast-flattening English vowels would be further affected by the shrieking, belly-flopping scallywags from the suburbs. 'What a toffee accent,' the kids would say. How confusing. After all, I rarely ate toffee. Treacle, maybe. It was years before I discovered the meaning of 'toff'.

At friends' backyard pools, my thick curly hair would be capped so tightly that my eyes were drawn back like slits and, as my ears were also covered, everything sounded muffled, as if I were under water. Which I rarely was as I didn't know how to swim.

During those Brighton Beach holidays in England, I splashed about and collected shells but swimming lessons didn't enter the equation and by the time I hit Canberra and, later, Parramatta, I didn't know the Australian crawl from a baby's rattle. As for that term 'breast stroke', it sounded too scandalous to be true.

Being mortified by my awful secret, I invented the most elaborate of excuses to get out of school swimming periods. Earaches, head colds, sore throats: young Susan pretended to suffer the lot as she sat in the stands watching her classmates frolicking as sleekly and smoothly as dolphins. Eventually, an observant teacher took me aside and said that if I met her after school, she would teach me how to swim.

Which she did, and it was heaven, apart from the regulation cap and the endless list of do's and don'ts from my mother. The first sudden rush of chlorine up my nose, the ecstasy of pushing against the water and moving up and down the pool as if slicing through satin. Later, boisterous high jinks at the school pool: pushing pals in the deep end, swimming through each other's legs, doing handstands and sneaking upside-down looks at the curious bumps in the boys' skin-tight Speedos.

'Susan!' It was Kristy, the aquarobics teacher, summoning my attention to the first exercise, which seemed to involve Cossack dancing under water. Faster, faster. Disco music pumped from a boom-box the size of an overnight bag. 'Let's travel!' yelled Kristy.

Travel? Hey, wait for me. In a long, wobbly conga line we started advancing through the water as Kristy ran alongside the pool. The women in cossies with skirts looked like sodden ballerinas as the pleated folds floated upwards and from side to side. Big, meaty arms flapped like fairy wings and there was the occasional girlish pirouette. In the water, we all felt weightless and the fattest of females were moving like sea sprites, their laughter high and ringing.

With the absence of mirrors or an audience, these aqua exercisers were gloriously unselfconscious. In their minds, they were 20 years younger and several sizes smaller as they arched and dived and embraced the water. On land they may have been the butt of beached-whale jokes, but in the pool they were synchronised mermaids.

There was an hour of working out with kickboards, hopping backwards, hoisting ourselves through rubber rings, underwater cycling and star jumps. The water became churned and frothy with our activity. Kristy gave us a cheer and dispensed cold drinks all round. 'You're a natural in the water,' she told me, with a pat on my shoulder. Her smile was soft and comforting and a shaft of sunlight beamed through the door to the swimming shed, like a benediction.

•

Graeme took time out from gardening on Saturday and Sunday afternoons during the football season. He'd install himself in front of one of Thistle Do's three televisions (our viewing tastes don't always coincide) and barrack his beloved Carlton Blues AFL team. I'd be in my office, tapping away on the keyboard, when suddenly the cry would come from the lounge room in a voice as strangled and frustrated as Victor Meldrew in the Brit soap 'One Foot in the Grave'. 'I don't believe it!' he'd yell in trademark Meldrew style. Then there'd be a thwack as the nearest thing to hand—usually a magazine, luckily—hit the screen.

Being from Melbourne, apparently barracking is in his blood. As I was brung up nice, as they say, well away from Aussie Rules territory, I missed out on the barracking gene. Perhaps the odd 'Jolly good show!' at the polo, according to Graeme.

Years ago, I wrote a newspaper column about that great Melbourne institution of chiacking. Unfortunately, without consultation, a sub-editor who thought I'd penned a very offbeat travel column changed the word throughout to kayaking. The paper's readers were startled to discover the little-known fact that C.J. Dennis had all but invented kayaking and his characters indulged in it with hearty regularity.

'Vulgar banter, coarse invective,' according to Dennis, which just about sums up Graeme in barracking mode, equipped with navy-blue-and-white bobble cap and scarf. The furniture would be moved about at Thistle Do so he could perform victory dances or chiack the players, calling them by words not taught to me in girlhood elocution classes. The worst chiacking would be reserved for his own team: if they let down their number one barracker by missing a mark or a goal, he'd refer to them in far worse language than he would the opposition. After all, the other lot were hopeless from the start.

When Graeme and I drove down to Sydney for a Swans game, he was appalled by the lack of inventiveness among barrackers. 'Swans supporters,' he muttered to me, 'just don't sufficiently *resent* the players when they stuff up.'

Writer Tom Keneally once said that Melbourne 'seems to be a secret to which you can obtain the code only if you are born into it or undergo a long initiation'. But Keneally has a code of his own. He's a legendary Manly-Warringah rugby league supporter and apparently can barrack effortlessly in Latin, having made it a mission to convert all the standard taunts to the language of scholars.

At the Bay, last winter, we were restricted to English, loud and hot, and, it not being the boating season, no sign of a kayak in which to cool off.

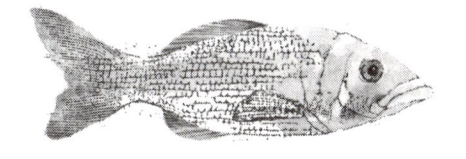

CHAPTER SIX

Some of My Friends Have Beaks

> *Behold the duck*
> *It does not cluck.*
> *A cluck it lacks.*
> *It quacks.*
> *It is specially fond*
> *Of a puddle or pond.*
> *When it dines or sups,*
> *It bottoms up.*
>
> Ogden Nash

Within hours of our moving into Thistle Do, the resident clan of kookaburras had come to check us out. Their investigation was tentative at first, conducted from a not-too-nosy distance on the power wires and the front fence of the next door neighbour. About a dozen of them sat in a line, opening and closing their beaks like those side-show plaster clowns with rotating heads into whose mouths fair-goers pitch little balls to win a prize. The noise was remarkable as they cackled away fit to burst.

When I arrived from England in the late 1950s and settled with my family in Canberra, there were a few resident kookaburras in our big, spidery Red Hill garden. The first time I heard them burst into their trademark laughing-jackass song, I screamed with alarm. I'd been brought up in mannered, holly-hedged Surrey amid polite birds who'd twitter away in the style of matrons taking tea at the vicarage. In comparison, the Canberra kookaburras sounded like banshees and had an unerring habit of appearing on cue to witness my many mishaps. Like a Greek chorus, they'd laugh and chatter their comments as I tripped on my skipping rope or toppled during a game of hopscotch or got sprayed by the rotating garden sprinkler.

'The birds are not really afraid,' wrote D.H. Lawrence, wonderingly, of Aussie bush birds in *Kangaroo*. And the lack of timidity of the Canberra kookas was to prove useful. Lady Prudence, my cat, was a birder, although she was regularly diverted from hunting by being dressed in doll's clothes and pushed around in a pram as a substitute for the little sister I didn't have. Aside from a failure to keep her tail from springing out under a frilled petticoat, she was beautifully obedient.

When she did go on the prowl and was about to get her dainty little teeth into a slow bird, the kookaburras would tilt their heads skywards and go off in rousing great chuckles and the rescued target would fly to safety. We bought her a collar with a little bell which also inhibited her strike rate. But Lady Prudence was not to be easily outwitted and somehow contrived to remove it and place it in the exact spot on our crescent driveway where my father would drive over it. Sure enough, one of the tyres smashed the bell. We didn't have the heart to replace it and thereafter relied on the kookas to keep watch while she hunted.

Lady Prudence had no idea that she'd been bestowed with a very aristocratic name in the hope her behaviour would be faultless, in a style befitting the resident mog at a one-time embassy. My father was a Canberra correspondent for the Sydney *Sun-Herald* at the time; he'd been posted from London to the federal parliamentary press gallery and we lived in what was known as the White House at 20 Mugga Way. It was owned by the Fairfax publishing house and had been the American Embassy, a fact we were reminded of each night as we sat at a long, polished dining table—about the length of a cricket pitch from child's-eye level—with the American eagle peering down at us from a tall stained-glass window.

At first, I was convinced the hard-eyed eagle was watching me, forever alert to table manners and dining indiscretions. So I chewed my vegetables in an exemplary way. But after I dropped my peas on several occasions and the eagle failed to react, I became bold enough to feed my dreaded Brussels sprouts to Lady Prudence under the table. The eagle didn't suddenly squawk like an alarm, as I'd imagined he might. Lady Prudence didn't eat the Brussels sprouts, of course, but rolled them around with her paw, like little balls. Sometimes she'd swipe one across the carpet and my father would look at the wobbly green missile and then at me but he never said a word. It was our exciting secret from Mother, who was a great one for green vegetables.

So by the time we settled into the Bay, the kookaburras held no mystery for me, although Graeme was occasionally alarmed at their outbursts. He sped the transition from inner-city urbanite to fully-fledged Coastie by acquiring a field guide to Australian birds, and the binoculars I'd bought for him to take to cricket and AFL matches began to do duty for bird-spotting.

But at first he scoffed as I cut meat for the kookaburras and placed it on the deck railings. I knew he was watching through the window but it took weeks for him to venture outside during morning and evening feeding times. As terrified as he was of spiders and snakes, I began to realise that the big, greedy kookas were scarier. They appeared to him as alien as invaders from outer space. Then one day as I walked back to Thistle Do from the shop, I saw him chopping meat and gingerly placing it out, leaping back a little as each of the kookaburras zoomed down from the trees.

Later, he confessed he'd been scared by the kookaburra clan which lives at Peacock Cottage. During his early-evening gardening sessions on the slopes, they would fly from the gum trees on the cliff across the road to branchy perches on the opposite side. When they landed it was sudden and skidding, like fighter planes coming to a halt on aircraft carriers. Swooping perilously low and cackling like witches on broomsticks, they often appeared to be about to land on his head or at least leave what Mother would have called 'a message' in his hair. He soon realised why many gardeners at the Bay favour broad-brimmed floppy hats that may not be the last word in sartorial elegance but do provide a defence against bird doings.

One neighbour at Thistle Do has an old bathroom basin in the middle of his backyard. It stands under a low-hanging branch and is hardly the height of garden chic but we soon realised it served as a kookaburra bathhouse. The birds would line up along the branch, as if queued at a public pool to dive off the tower. One by one they'd fly in, paddle about in the collected rainwater, shake their wings and zoom off. There was such a synchronicity about their movements it was if someone just out of frame was blowing a whistle and timing each dip. Space for a birdbath was immediately drawn into Graeme's garden plans for the extended Peacock Cottage.

Opinion seems to be divided at the Bay about whether to feed the birds. City exiles, like me, tend to become so excited about living in such a birdy place that we rush in with cubed meat and seed because we want to encourage the kookas and parrots to stay.

We are, in fact, upsetting the natural order of things and I'm not sure I would have set up such a well-stocked takeaway food outlet for birds if I'd thought the matter through.

Within a few months, we could recognise certain kookaburras at Thistle Do by their feeding habits, their degree of skittishness and even, in the case of Fluffy and Scruffy, by their coats. These two became almost like pets and we worried about Scruffy when he'd disappear for days at a time. When he returned, feathers all askew and on one occasion with cuts around his neck as if he'd done battle with barbed-wire, we celebrated by chopping him some steak. Sirloin! We were certifiably mad by this stage.

Our friends Frank and Jill Mullens live in a Sydney harbourfront apartment at McMahons Point and when I rang one morning, Jill airily told me that Frank was unable to come to the phone because he was dicing fillet steak for an off-course kookaburra who'd taken up residence amid their Italian patio furniture. After that I felt less silly about my gourmet provisioning, although Graeme became fond of telling everyone how I cut up a couple of prime ribs for Scruffy when he appeared after one of his derring-do absences. I'd thought Graeme was staying at Surry Hills that night and figured the meat would go off—I don't eat beef and the ribs had been in the fridge at least two days. But Graeme decided to drive to the Bay and arrived with the announcement that he was going to make me an omelette and barbecue the beef for himself. Too late: omelettes all round; eaten on the deck with Scruffy and Fluffy looking on.

That night Graeme, made even more creatively chatty after a reviving glass of red wine or six, decided to rename Scruffy as Ricky after Australian cricketer Ponting (bad haircut, he explained; later Ponting ended up with a black eye after a Sydney nightclub scrap which pleased Graeme no end as poor old Scruffy frequently looked as if he'd had a hard night on the tiles). Then he remarked that Fluffy looked like President Bill Clinton—again it was the hair that decided it. Fluffy had a bouffant top, not unlike Slick Willy's nuke-proof quiff. What Fluffy was getting up to in his spare time we had no idea but Graeme insisted the Slick Willy tag had to stay. Fluffy and Scruffy, too full of the Woy Woy Butchery's best beef to move, watched us sleepily from the deck's railing. If kookaburras could lick their chops, they would have done so that evening.

One summer's twilight when Thistle Do felt like a wood-fired oven, we sat outside listening to the cricket which was turned up full volume on the lounge-room TV. The Sri Lankans were batting well in a One Day Game but seemed unlikely to catch the Aussie team's score. It would have been appropriate if our Ricky Ponting had turned up at that moment but it was another kookaburra who appeared at Graeme's feet, holding what appeared to be a mouse in his beak. Thwack, thwack, the bird beat his prey from side to side as Graeme and I screamed, both leaping onto our sun-chairs. I told Graeme that it was a...rat!

We were about to run indoors when I noticed the rodent had a pink satin tail. It was a baby's toy, a pink-grey stuffed mouse with startled glass eyes and straw whiskers. The kookaburra flew onto a branch, continued to bash the mouse—he must have had jaw-ache by then as it was a very round toy—and when he accidentally dropped it onto the front lawn, he swooped down, retrieved it and landed back on our deck.

The poor bird went through a crisis of indecision. While he was sitting there with this huge but not very flavoursome snack in his beak, Scruffy, Fluffy and the gang were busy feasting on the diced beef I'd just served in their trays for what we'd come to call the Flocktail Hour. He hopped across and tried to work out how he could help himself to some meat while not letting go of his trophy. The other birds greeted him with great cackles and in the end he flew away. Later that evening, as I locked the sliding glass door out to the deck, I could see the bird in silhouette on the power wire—he still had the stuffed toy wedged in his beak.

The kookaburras are the rowdiest but the galahs and rainbow lorikeets are the most common of Bay birds—about as special as sparrows, in fact. The galahs are the bossiest of all, and watching their antics on the feeding tray I attached on a wooden arm to the deck I have learned the real meaning of 'pecking order'. Galahs are big birds who seem to favour travelling in pairs, at least where morning and evening food forays are concerned. When they come in to land on the feeding tray, they raise their grey wings, revealing pink breasts, soft and rosy, like reflected sunsets. But good manners rarely accompany their girlish prettiness. Using their wings as we would elbows, they simply nudge away any rainbow lorikeets that may have been in residence. The galahs' combs rise, too, when in fighting mode, giving them the appearance of punk rockers with freshly gelled Mohawks. Graeme likens their pink-and-grey colour scheme to a One Day Cricket uniform so we often refer to them as Team Galah.

The rainbow lorikeets hang upside down on the power wires, like circus performers, and screech at the bully-boy galahs. The artist Ferdinand Bauer painted a pair of rainbow lorikeets, one with wings extravagantly outstretched, as part of the 2000-strong collection of natural history artworks he was commissioned to produce in his role as artist to the British ship *Investigator*, despatched to map the coast of Australia in the early 1800s. Apparently he colour-coded his drawings and did the actual painting much later. Certainly, it's almost impossible to recall the exact composition of a rainbow lorikeet's coat, so bright and blurred. Back in London, with sparrows and pigeons, all bundles of fulvous feathers, huddled on his windowsill, Bauer must surely have wondered if he hadn't simply imagined the explosive colours of Australian birdlife.

Soon these Bauer birds are joined by their cousins, the eastern rosellas, with their pretty white cheeks and blue outer-tail feathers, and by crested pigeons, their topknots straight and stiff, like little flagpoles. Then mynah birds with their saffron-coloured beaks and eyes as bright and hard as boiled yellow lollies. All waiting their turns. If the galahs settle in for too long, I put slices of multi-grain bread along the deck railing and clouds of rainbow lorikeets descend, their beaks busily pecking out the seeds.

When we took a short holiday to Port Douglas in North Queensland and stayed at Thala Beach Lodge, a new wilderness resort owned by our friends Rob and

Oonagh Prettejohn, there were rainbow lorikeets galore. The lodge has an open-sided dining pavilion set high in the trees like a rondavel at an African safari camp. At the next table one breakfast, a German couple asked us to take their photo with the feathery throngs and said their trip to Australia had been made complete by seeing these native birds of 'impossible colours'. It reminded me of a slogan that the 100% Mambo surf-wear makers once used in their advertising: 'colours to rock the retina'. More poetically, Dame Agatha Christie, who visited Australia in 1922, wrote in her autobiography of 'great clustering swarms' of birds with wonderful colours, 'like flying jewels'.

I had been trying to persuade one of our rainbow lorikeets—note the 'our', how ridiculously proprietorial I'd become—to sit on my head. Some mornings I'd imagine I really could tell them apart, which was pretty silly as they all wear the same clown's costume—dark blue head, yellow-green collar, jaffa-orange breast, violet-blue belly, tangerine under the wing and a gorgeous red beak. I wanted one on my hair so I could have my photo taken and send it to my school chum, Peggy, who now lives at Maroochydore on the Queensland Sunshine Coast. In the mid-60s when we were at junior high school, we went on a motoring holiday with my parents from Sydney to the Gold Coast.

The highlight of the trip was a visit to the Currumbin Bird Sanctuary where we were snapped with rainbow lorikeets in our hair as we held out plates of honeyed

some of my friends have beaks 119

seeds. I'd changed my name to Jodie and Peggy became Nicky because it seemed obvious you'd be called something like that if you were in an episode of 'Gidget', which we pretended we were.

In the photo, my holiday mop-top (it was the era of the Beatles), has been scraped back by Mother's best bristle brush in readiness for a cut. Looming was my strict ladies college with its rules about seemly hairstyles. Jodie knew summer was over and the game was up when those scissors came out.

The photo was taken by the official photographer at Currumbin which was just as well as my parents treated cameras as things of mystery and frequently shook nervously when pressing the button. Judging by the mounted snaps—square little ones, mostly black-and-white, not like today's panoramas and lavish enlargements—in leather-bound albums, my childhood passed as a blur, with the small Susan frequently appearing as a ghostly double-edged spectre.

•

For years, I have collected ducks of all sizes and materials, loving their aerodynamic shape and pertness. On the surface, ducks are so serene and unruffled, while below the water their little legs work like crazy. It's always seemed a metaphor for my life: trying to keep a calm facade while underneath all is panic. Several of my friends have dubbed me the Grand Duchess and continue to give me ducky cards and presents, all of which have had to be kept at the Surry Hills apartment or on my office desk, Peacock Cottage and Thistle Do being so awash with fish and mermaids.

When Graeme and I were courting (the will-he-won't-he dating period lasted about a month; he'd made up his mind to marry me, apparently, during our first weekend away, to Kims Resort at Toowoon Bay), he said he'd buy me a real duck one day. I didn't like to put him off by revealing what I knew about ducks and their destructive habits. In the same category as Ogden Nash's canaries, really, who 'when they're moulting, they're pretty revolting'.

But now, we had the next best thing—a pair of mallards. These community ducks waddled past the muddy mangroves and shoreline scrub of the Bay up to Thistle Do each evening, feeding handsomely on bread of varying degrees of freshness and gourmet standard. I told a guest one lunchtime that their preference was high-top toast-slice white and when she looked at me incredulously, Graeme commented that I'd gone quackers. She managed a tight smile.

The ducks are known as Charles and Camilla, so named according to a neighbour because the female is so plain. Not a charitable gesture, but the names have stuck. Charles has a splendid glossy green head and a white ring around his neck and a burnished brown bib but Camilla is mottled in a nondescript beige sort of way. In fashion terms, he is the equivalent of colour-clashing Florida leisurewear but she's about as modish as a beige trouser suit.

When Graeme's mother, Jean, and his stepfather, Bill, came to stay at Christmas, towing their caravan along the coastal route from Melbourne, the ducks introduced themselves on their first evening. Up the three low steps to the caravan they climbed and then quacked at Jean until she found some bread. The ducks seemed delighted at this new arrangement, as if the caravan were a mobile food van especially parked in our front garden for their convenience. When Jean and Bill left after their two-week holiday, Charles and Camilla were most put out. Once more, it was a matter of me throwing the bread from the deck or, on one occasion when the phone rang as I started their feeding and then I chatted for too long, they climbed our stairs, strutted through the open door and stood expectantly by my feet.

The gardens of Thistle Do and Peacock Cottage are also patrolled by brush turkeys. The males have large yellow wattles which look like Elizabethan ruffs and bare red heads and the females, as is the bird kingdom's way, are less colourful and smaller. Alfredo had been making amorous advances to one of the girl brush turkeys behind Peacock Cottage, doing his 'tail acting' as Graeme called it, but she wouldn't have anything to do with him. The ultimate brush off, perhaps.

The brush turkeys at Thistle Do take late-afternoon constitutionals along the dirt track and are never in any rush to move aside when cars come along. They step high and seem quite particular about where to put their feet. They remind me of parsons promenading unhurriedly, usually in pairs, discussing important matters, hands clasped behind. But that's when they are at their most appealing—less so early in the morning when they decide to walk on Thistle Do's tin roof. The house is built into a steep slope at the back and juts out over a single garage and on stilts in front. So the brush turkeys can virtually step off the ridge and onto the roof as a very convenient short cut to the front deck. The first time we heard them we presumed, naturally, as we'd just moved from the big, bad city, that burglars were about to break in. It was about five in the morning and we tiptoed out to the loungeroom, ready to grab for the phone. Then through the windows we saw two great black blobs topple off the roof, grunting heavily—hardly with the graceful bounce of ninja bandits.

Another day we watched a grevillea in Thistle Do's front garden shake so much we thought a child must be hiding in it. As we approached, a flurry of honeyeaters rose into the sky. They had been busily feeding on the bush's nectar, wriggling and bouncing to get their beaks nice and deep.

Now we're used to all sorts of rustlings and calls and sometimes we're unaware just how much intrusive background noise is going on. One Sunday morning while doing a live phone interview for a radio station at Newcastle, further up the Coast, the announcer suddenly cut in and asked me why there was so much racket. Well, I told her, Fluffy and Scruffy were at the window talking to each other (I restrained myself from referring to them as Ponting and Clinton) and the rainbow lorikeets were screeching because the galahs were hogging all the seed and there was a brush turkey on the roof above my study practising its boot scooting. Luckily, the call wasn't taking place at Peacock Cottage or Alfredo would have got into the act. When he's in full cry, I doubt you'd need satellite dishes to hear him in Newcastle.

•

Just before we moved to the Bay Graeme's elder daughter, Nellie, gave us a terracotta bird feeder with a wooden rail and a chain by which to hang it. Months later, when we finally unpacked all the boxes piled in the garage, we found it and installed it under the deck's awning. Curiously shaped and curved, almost like an Ottoman helmet, it had been discovered by Nellie at Sydney's Paddington Markets. We wondered if it wasn't a bit too exotic for the Bay birds because even though we filled it with seed, they ignored it. When the galahs had taken over the feeder tray and the rainbow lorikeets and eastern rosellas and crested pigeons were in line, still they ignored the hanging hat. Then one morning, a pair of Australian king parrots arrived. The male of the species has a scarlet head and breast and a very long tail while

some of my friends have beaks *125*

the female's head is a lovely lime green and so is her decolletage until it merges into a hot red-orange.

They made straight for Nellie's hanging feeder, confidently perching one on each side, heads dipping in and out of the tray as if operated by clockwork. They stayed all summer and into autumn, arriving twice a day and showing a marked preference for the pricier Trill parrot mix over Home Brand all-sorts.

When they departed, the smaller rainbow lorikeets commandeered the feeder as their own. The openings each side were large enough for them to step inside so all that was visible on the exterior were their green tail-feathers bobbing about. On rainy days, at least one of these birds would take up residence in the feeder, occasionally poking out his red beak and blue head for a weather update.

•

Father James Murray, the religious affairs editor at the *Australian*, has moved to Baulkham Hills in Sydney's so-called 'garden district'. To describe the new home he shares with his godson, Lawrence, the epithet fits. They have a deep garden as green and lush as the Emerald Isle from which James's ancestors hail. Great white waves of sulphur-crested cockatoos descend onto the railings of their broad timber deck each morning and James arrives at the office with embellished tales of the feeding patterns and quaint behaviour of his feathered flock. We frequently swap bird stories as if discussing the mild eccentricities of our close relatives, much to the amusement of colleagues.

He asked me to buy him a camera duty-free on my way to Hong Kong and Istanbul—not just to take snaps during his annual pilgrimage to Europe but so he could photograph the Baulkham Hills birdlife. I bought him an Olympus, a few models up the super-duper scale from my own. After a few practice attempts, with the ever-patient Lawrence deciphering the instruction leaflet, James was all action. Rolls and rolls of bird prints were developed—cockatoos from all known angles, photographed with the precision of a David Attenborough doco. He gave me a few for my office noticeboard and I pinned them next to Fluffy and Scruffy. (Graeme still insisted their names were Ricky and Slick Willy but I was determined to stick with the cosy Beatrix Potter approach. He said if I could get the birds indoors, I'd have them dressed in waistcoats and wellington boots and starring in pop-up books. I've never told him about Lady Prudence's pram-bound adventures.)

Most journalists at the *Australian* have photos of children on their desks: even gay staff seem to manage the odd niece or nephew. My sons are about the same age as Lachlan Murdoch, son of Rupert, now News Limited's chairman, and, given the youthist culture pervading the media, I decided it would be a bad idea to have current photos of twentysomething Justin and Joe on my desk. No use advertising the fact I'm an old bat who's been around since the era of pterodactyls, so I brought in pictures of the boys in their Cub Scout uniforms, circa 1980.

There they sit between Roja, the little Indian girl I sponsor through World Vision, and my young godchildren, Laura and Sebastian. All those children are pinned up in gallery style amid Father James's cockatoos and myriad Bay birds (no pterodactyls) and I'm sure Murdoch Minor would be enthralled by the fully cool desk of this nature nymph if he were to saunter past.

•

Charles Swancott, the Coast's historian, has written about Harry Pickett, a member of the founding family of Kincumber. As a boy, Harry longed to fly and was particularly entranced by seagulls and pelicans. He'd try to count the movements of their wings and flapped his arms as he ran alongside the water. He collected bags of feathers and glued them thickly onto the canvas he had stretched over a bamboo framework. The contraption was secured to his arms with loops of fencing wire. 'He mounted a ladder to the barn roof and stood ready for the plunge,' Swancott wrote. 'While his adoring parents, grandparents, sisters and brothers waited, he waved a cheery goodbye to all and with arms outspread leaped into space... He fell, fortunately into a plum tree below the barn. Only his pride was hurt, and his mother's arms soon soothed the bitterness of failure.'

The Picketts were an interesting family, if folklore is to be believed: one Paul was born without eyelids and rolled his eyes backwards to go to sleep, and the matriarch of the clan was the first woman in the Brisbane Water district to 'adopt the use of men's trousers for bush work and horse-back riding'. Swancott made the claim that the Picketts have more descendants in the area than any of the other early families, and they're immortalised on the apostrophe-free map at Picketts Valley.

As I read these tales aloud to Graeme on the deck of Thistle Do, there was an explosion of galahs. A car had backfired and the birds scattered in a great whirring cloud. We toasted the ghost of Harry Pickett with a sunset shandy as the galahs swept back to the branches, their wings moving slow and pink and even.

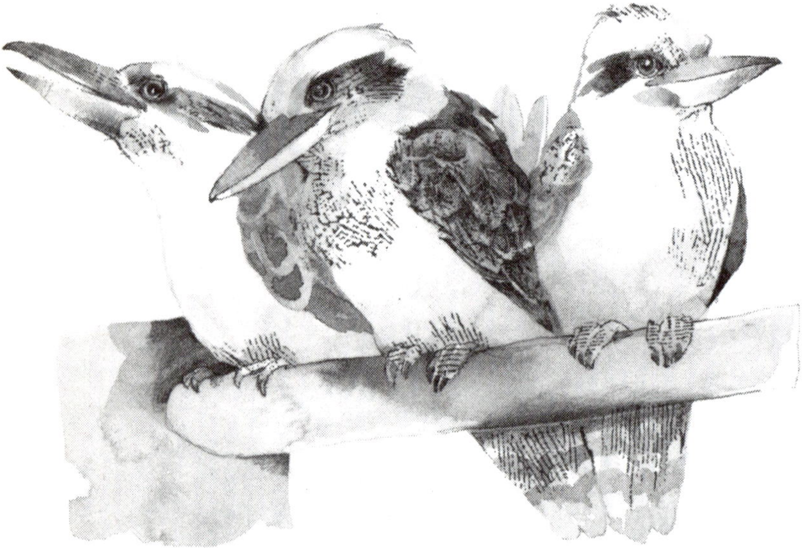

Kookaburras

The kookaburra is the largest of the kingfisher family and, aside from the pelican, which really is in an airship-like league of its own, is one the biggest birds to be commonly found at the Bay. It has a long beak, black on top and horn-coloured below, and its markings are brown and creamy-white, with the male often displaying a blue patch on its rump. It tends to home in on its target—in our case, the feeding bowls on the sundeck—like a little fighter pilot, its tail standing up in rather a pert fashion when it lands. Kookaburras are very useful as snake catchers and also make quick work of rodents and lizards. Its raucous call sounds like laughter: one group member begins a low chuckle and the rest start cackling. The kookaburra makes a perfect wake-up alarm—if you want to be roused at five, that is. No wonder it's known as 'the bushman's clock'.

CHAPTER SEVEN

Fibrocitis

'The shack is the architectural equivalent of the battered ute with a mongrel in the back...If your shack doesn't leak, it's not worthy of the name. It's a holiday house.'

James Cockington

Graeme waved the *Sydney Morning Herald*'s 'Domain' lift-out in front of my nose. James Cockington had written a charming piece about Aussie shack culture. 'I told you they were shacks, not cottages,' said Graeme, a little too triumphantly.

I loved the idea of a shed-like shack. But I didn't want to live permanently in one. The shack that exists in the nostalgic imagination of my generation is for uncomplicated weekends and holidays only. 'The spirit of the shack had to be right,' wrote Robert Drewe of his character David's search for a Central Coast weekender in his short story 'The Bodysurfers', 'its character set preferably somewhere in the 1950s. It would need a properly casual, even run-down, beach air. It would have a veranda to sleep weekend guests, a working septic system, an open fireplace and somewhere to hang a dartboard.'

The mock-Caribbean style of Peacock Cottage was a little too bourgeois and geographically incorrect to suit the shack ideal. But its vernacular, I argued with Graeme, could be termed seaside universal. It was made to accommodate crackling heat and trails of sand and the colours we'd chosen echoed bay, beach and bush. With its secretive wooden shutters and polished surfaces, it suited me perfectly. I longed for our extension plans to be approved so we could actually move in.

But our rented Thistle Do was not far short of a shack. Fibro, badly ventilated, with small rooms and low ceilings, it had the appeal of a small oven on summer days, especially late afternoon when the sun hammered its pale blue facade. Anyone who waxes adjectival about shacks has never spent too long in one, all but camping amid 'cracked plates and rejected bedspreads, and hung about with ill-fitting fly-wire doors', as Adelaide writer Kerryn Goldsworthy has put it. There's nothing romantic about the square, squat fibro vernacular, save for its endangered status.

But such architecture suits the Coast completely, enhancing its aspic-set quality, fitting in with utes in the driveways, old fishing piers and little shops selling bait and tackle. Occasionally you see some clever makeovers, with decks built in empathy, sliding wood-framed doors replacing mean windows and jaunty nautical blinds replacing rainbow-coloured venetians for a chic beach-cottage look.

But the newer beach developments eschew fibro completely. Up on Killcare Heights overlooking the Bay, there's been an outbreak of brick veneer-eal disease. In the past year, prime building blocks have sprouted mausoleum-sized homes, as brutal as fortresses atop precipitous inclines. Mother Mary says the Killcare Heights folk usually prefer brick because fibro or wood feels too flimsy against the big southerly busters which blow up on muggy afternoons. 'Prestige Brick' trumpet the For Sale signs, but there's an inappropriateness to some of the architecture that's almost breathtaking.

With its easy lifestyle and cheap housing, the Coast is popular with retirees. Plant nursery signs energetically advertise those herbs that are good for creaky conditions: 'Here now! Pennywort for arthritis!' The many front-parlour beauticians and 'hair stylistes' who operate out of their homes list pensioner prices for permanent waves and rinses (perhaps the wisteria tone so beloved of Dame Edna) although often there'll be a weekly special chalked up. It was half-price dreadlocks one week outside one such salon in Woy Woy. I envisaged a line of cost-conscious grannies, swinging their new beaded plaits as they made their way up to the Housie Hall.

To cope with the influx of retirement-age residents, there has been a lot of villa development, often contained in community-style enclaves, with security triumphing over style. At Ettalong, I have noticed a compound of what appear to be demountable cabins, looking unfortunately like kennels but made jolly with proprietorial flourishes such as hanging baskets and striped awnings. They look snug enough but are set stiflingly close together, shoulder-to-shoulder, as if on parade.

The nearby St Huberts Island is almost a gated community, reached via its own bridge. It was built in the 1970s when the Hooker development group subdivided the island as a residential corral, against much opposition. The exclamatory architectural styles range from Counterfeit Tudor and Chinese Embassy to Italianate Mansion and what could only be termed Spec Builder Experimental. The idea is to boast, not blend.

Some of the newer and boxier pastel designs on St Huberts, all variations on a theme, could have been transplanted from the Gold Coast's Sanctuary Cove estate. In fact the whole feel is very Surfers Paradise, but in the case of St Huberts it's surrounded by wide waterways rather than threaded with man-made canals. Lawns are as pressed as hotel laundry and roller-doors come in pairs. A few old cottages remain, laced with choko vines and budgies in cages hung on the verandah. Hunkered down behind the mangroves, they seem to be hanging their heads in shame.

St Huberts is a distant cry from its previous life when it was Bird Island, a simple, swampy isle at the entrance to Cockle Creek. Its first resident was a Catholic priest, Father Cornelius Coughlan, who settled there in 1843, cleared a portion of the mangrove-riddled land and started a 'luxuriant' banana plantation, believed to be the first on the Coast. He would row across to his Holy Cross Church at Kincumber, and to parishioners further afield, perhaps sustained by the odd banana as he went. After his death, the island was sold several times, most notably to a Mr Kinnane who tried, no one quite knows why, to breed possums but failed due to a paucity of the right variety of gum trees.

Local historian Charles Swancott wrote of early settlers building their homes of 'wattle and daub, slabs or sandstone'. 'They fashioned rough tables, benches, bed and shelves from round bush timber,' he recounted, 'smoothed up with the broad axe; their tool handles were also shaped from selected bush timber.' We like to think of a strange continuum at Peacock Cottage, as Phil makes our furniture by hand, always from recycled timber, and our ferry windows creak along their tracks, no longer lashed and salted with sea spray but rattling and protesting against Sydney's heavy summer rains.

Fibro still rules through Woy Woy and Ettalong, and those houses available for holiday rentals or used as weekenders are immediately apparent by their low-maintenance gardens and depressingly unattractive metal roll-a-blinds hiding the windows, as if the house is in convalescence. The majority of permanent residents tweezer their lawns and cultivate their pots as though in the running for a Tidy Town award. Weekenders invariably have little more than a low-maintenance clump of hydrangeas, an oleander bush and sometimes old rusty tins or a cut-off 44-gallon drum planted with sandy geraniums.

And almost always a frangipani tree. 'Frannies' grow like beanstalks on the Coast and not just in the usual creamy-yellow but a variety with a pink flower the colour of a little girl's birthday cake icing or ballet tutu. When the petals fall, they do so in such profusion it looks as if someone has been recklessly pulling apart Hawaiian flower leis and scattering them to the breeze.

House names speak of long-ago loyalties (Torquay, Polperro, Bognor Regis) or of wishful thinking (Sausalito, Capri, Acapulco). When Coast identity Henry Robert Cox II married Ethel McDowell in 1883, they spent a luxurious three years on honeymoon touring the world, including, daringly for the day, Japan. They then named their Woy Woy house Kirei, or 'pretty' in Japanese.

But Aussie larrikinism is apparent, too: Emoh Ruo is popular, as are Avarest, Weona, Tolofin, Seldomin, Dunwerkin, Dunroamin, Dunmovin and Goodenough. Krowdrah looks suitably exotic until one reads it backwards. I spent days driving around looking, unsuccessfully, for a Wyewurk. That was the name of the real bungalow at Thirroul on the New South Wales South Coast where D.H. Lawrence and his wife stayed in the 1920s. But in his novel *Kangaroo* it became the less self-conscious Coo-ee (although the Sydney house rented by *Kangaroo*'s Richard and Harriet Somers was the jocular Torestin). Lawrence was specific about the use of the word bungalow, which is one I've always liked. It comes from the Hindi for a single-storey house and, given our rampaging rajahs and pavonine sound effects, I wondered if it wouldn't be a better tag than cottage.

Graeme informed me that bungalow was a word that fairly stank of the red-roofed suburbs. Then he told me of people ordering bungalow, instead of bangalow, palms from the local nursery, and being told by the always-laconic blokes behind the counter that they were right out of 'single storey palms'.

There followed a discussion of decks. At least we both agreed that Peacock Cottage's big wide platform was a deck, but around the Bay, we discovered our neighbours had other ideas. One called our deck a drawbridge, so tall did it sit up the cliff. The two Pauls spoke of their lanai, a word I love. It's an Hawaiian word meaning terrace, specifically for the serving thereon of fruit daiquiris, if my extended stays on Maui could be counted as evidence.

'Lanais, bungalows, drawbridges, daiquiris,' muttered Graeme as he mixed us each a shandy at Thistle Do. He had decided to start a movement for the preservation of the beer-and-lemonade shandy, considering it a quintessential Aussie tipple and perfect for drinking in one's shack. 'Sea shandies' he called them, idly wondering if instead of being remembered for baring his bottom as Alvin Purple, he might become renowned for his pale amber brews, served during the Flocktail Hour by the Bay.

All through Ettalong, street names herald holiday. Picnic Parade takes you into town and the flat waterfront and then a fishing theme takes hook—roads rejoice in such names as Bream, Whiting, Flounder, Schnapper and Flathead. When I interviewed the Australian Brandenburg Orchestra's artistic director, Paul Dyer, for my last book, *Places in the Heart*, he spoke of Ettalong holidays, remembering the surge of excitement as they arrived, from Sydney's northern suburbs, at this 'foreign place' with its different shops and exotic summer fruit, like mangoes, paw-paws, rockmelons and passionfruit.

'We returned to the same cottage three times,' he told me. 'It was fibro, it had a lawn, a hideous gate, a front fence with crisscrossed wire, like an institution. It was a box, really, but it had quite a lot of rooms. There were two lounge rooms: one was skimpily covered with new but very thin carpet and the other had old-fashioned patterned lino of the sort that gathers every bit of dirt. There was a mulberry bush in the garden and the fruit would be on the ground, so often we trailed into the house with mucky purple feet.' Instant Ettalong in the 1960s and the description still applies, in part, as we are hurtled into the next century.

At Ocean Beach, Umina, the *Australian Women's Weekly* 'Holiday Home of the Year' for 1956 still stands strong, its nautical lines and timber decks hung with life belts now having become sufficiently retro to represent the height of fashion. 'Designed like a ship!' exclaimed an August 1957 magazine article. The original owners are still in residence, recently quoted by a local Coast newspaper as saying the best thing about living in the flat-roofed two-storey house is that it feels like being on a cruise ship 'without being seasick'.

Ettalong and Woy Woy gardens are still homes to bands of gnomes, as they were when Paul Dyer would 'wander down to the end of the street and not know what was around the corner'. But their safety has become an issue these days as the little fellows can fall prey to dastardly agents for the Garden Gnome Liberation Front. It's a French-based organisation which takes itself seriously enough to have international chapters, including one on the Coast. At certain times of the year, perhaps when the moon is full and wild dogs howl, gnome nabbers come out in force, rescuing the red-capped chaps from endlessly fishing in blue cement ponds and guarding wishing wells.

One female nabber went to court and was found guilty of possessing 35 garden ornaments stolen from the yards of her neighbours. The stash included two concrete snails, a wombat, a dog, a statue of a boy holding a birdbath, two flamingos, three Aborigines, a cast-iron wheel, a frog and two gnomes. The story made the international press; after two little plaster figures were found hung from a tree, concerned police in Brussels warning residents to 'bring their garden gnomes indoors at night'.

Apparently, it's not unusual for gnome nabbers to leave ransom notes. Usually, these do not demand money but deal with blackmail of the sort which suggests that if the gnome-owner doesn't de-kitsch their front garden (that statue of the Manikin Pis and the miniature Mykonos windmill can go for a start), then the whole kaboodle will be torched, and not by the fake Polynesian ceremonial fire-lights by the faux-Roman pool, either.

In New Zealand, the Kiwis have taken a curious slant on things by manufacturing Dead Dwarves which can be bought, in varying degrees of writhing repose, with a dagger in their back. Quite the rage, apparently, in the parterre gardens of Auckland's toney harbourside suburbs. Very troll, one could say.

But no such trollery in Normandy, where the Garden Gnome Liberation Front has as its clear mission to rid France of such kitschness as plaster toadstools, storks, butterflies and, of course, gnomes. The Front's tactics allegedly involve rounding up the offending gnomes in the dead of night and abandoning them in the woods, ideally in groups of seven, as a tribute to Snow White. Often, the little fellows are repainted with colours and designs more contemporary than your classic red cap, blue smock and brown breeches. Tracksuit stripes, number 23 Michael Jordan logos and sparkling disco make-up have been among the hip gnomester looks that have made it a tad tricky for owners to claim their loved ones at the local pound after police raids on the woods.

We have this rather misplaced notion that the French are more voguish and innately stylish than we are. The proliferation of gnomes in gardens from the shady arrondissements of Paris to the terraced hillsides of the Riviera would seem to put paid to this notion. What the French need as much as we do is a Minister for Style and Taste with a particular brief on community housing and gnomelessness. Penalties could be introduced for home-owners who didn't keep their front yards in shipshape condition—and by that, I don't mean models of boats made from empty beer bottles.

Writing in the late 1970s, Dennis Pryor observed that Australians are somewhat obsessed with garden 'featurism'. 'A house is not a home until it makes its presence felt in the world. "Stop, passer-by!" said Roman grave inscriptions, "and read this epitaph". But Australians cannot wait for the grave; they want their immortality now,' he wrote.

Some Coasties are clearly impatient for such fame. Plaster pelicans and seagulls stand on cement plinths, weather vanes are shaped like whales or dolphins, lifesaver rings hang from walls and old oars are stuck in gardens, sometimes with a bird-feeder tray on top. There's a nondescript brick house in Woy Woy with a folly attached to its front; it's a coralstone grotto, with niches holding statues of swans and native spearthrowers, and the whole affair just clings there, like a barnacle.

My father, Elwyn, and my stepmother, June, live on the Coast at Killarney Vale. It's a flat, sandy suburb on the way to The Entrance by way of Long Jetty—or Longevity as it's known by local wags, as a nod to the number of retired residents. He's a potterer of the highest order, always making things 'neat and tidy' in the garden and, when there's no one to stop him, whipping out a paintbrush and giving everything in his path a coat of nice white paint. Including June's terracotta pots and a pair of gnomes she'd been given as a present. The chaps were Italian-made, and about as witty in style as gnomes could ever get. When she returned from shopping one afternoon, Elwyn had painted them white and, with an artistic flourish, added little blue jackets and red caps.

June needed the proverbial cup of tea and a good lie-down after that episode, but not before she locked away Elwyn's brushes and tins of paint in the garden shed. On nights when the moon is full, I have visions of Elwyn creeping from garden to garden, perhaps in a burglar-like balaclava or face-stocking, whisking his brush over unsuspecting gnomes the length and breadth of Longevity.

•

Many of the older houses have fibro sleep-outs, separate little cabins to cope with peak-season overflow, a 1950s and '60s solution to the same problem encountered by the old Terrigal and Avoca guesthouses when they would have to erect holiday tents. They remind me of *garçonnières*, literally boys' houses, built by the French settlers at their grand plantation homes along the River Road between New Orleans and Baton Rouge, Louisiana. The boys of the house would be banished to sleep in these pavilions until they came of age. The subtext was that it kept the young masters away from the single women in the main house, although we can only guess how the black girls in the servants' quarters must have fared.

While cabins dot seaside backyards, the front is proudly reserved for many a flagpole. Hard to know if it's patriotism or pretentiousness involved in flying the Southern Cross, although voting preferences can be gathered by the number flown at half-mast to mark the deaths of Labor politicians Diamond Jim McClelland and Don Dunstan. A photograph of Empire Bay circa 1910 shows Charles Swinbourne's General Store, Post and Telephone Office with two Australian flags prominently aloft.

On Australia Day morning each year, the flag is raised in Turo Park at Pretty Beach, followed by a breakfast barbecue ('gold coin donation' suggested) and, that night, a bush dance, with music from the ilk of the appropriately named Blue Gum Band and Rolly Rushbrook. All proceeds to the renovations of the newly revamped Wagstaffe Hall, by the water near a handsome pine and across from the Wagstaffe Store where once I ducked in for an ice-cream cone and before being served asked an old-timer leaning in front of the counter if he was before me. Looking me up and down, he replied, with a slow smile, 'I'd say about forty years before you, love.'

•

When guests came to stay or for lunch, there'd be as much interest in looking at real estate as places of local interest. We played tour guides, zipping over to Terrigal where, in the 1960s, my friend Peggy and I stayed at the Florida Guesthouse and sneaked away one afternoon from my ever-vigilant mother to buy a can of hairspray at a nearby pharmacy. Gossamer Firm Hold, from memory, and it was the most contraband substance we could think of. We teased our hair to the approximate shape of industrial sewing machine bobbins and sat on twin beds in our small room across the hallway from my parents' grander suite. When my father walked in, we were singing 'I Wanna Hold Your Hand', using the hairspray can as a mike.

On the site where the Florida once stood there's the Crowne Plaza, a Holiday Inn painted in fairyland pink. It has good restaurants and sea-view rooms and much to offer families, but its arrival in 1989 as the then Peppers by the Sea meant the end of Terrigal's 'ocean village' status. New mansions with Federation verandahs and leadlight windows are proof horrendous of the historical dyslexia practised by developers who rejoice in building a house in 1990 in the style of 1909.

Waterview homes have hit the one-million-dollar mark and real-estate agents advertise properties built in 'Mediterranean contemporary style, with Greek columns' and tell prospective buyers that Terrigal has everything one could ever need, including soya milk lattes. The word 'Fediterranean' has begun to appear to describe Aussie bungs with a cross-cultural agenda of verandahs, deep hallways, stucco arches and wrought iron.

Want to buy in Ettalong? Be quick. 'God's not making any more land in Ettalong!' is the warning from one real-estate agent.

•

Mother Mary reports that the holiday-house market turns over every 10 years or so. That's the standard cycle for children growing up and the pattern of family holidays changing. But some weekenders in prized areas rival city prices. Even a bathing box—one of those candy-striped cabins you see on English beaches—sold for $185,000 at Melbourne's Portsea. I heard this report on Radio 2BL as I drove to Erina Fair, a leviathan shopping mall with all the accoutrements of its city counterparts, included piped music and spruikers advertising spot-specials.

The Bay has only the Old Killcare Store for smart snacks, home-made produce and caffeine fixes for the jitterati plus the all-purpose general store which functions as a cellars, post office and petrol station. The latter also has a small grocery section and used to sell take-away food, including Gordon's legendary Killie Burgers—and they almost did kill you, too, given they were so tall you just about broke your jaw trying to eat them. In the case of severe indigestion, there's the friendly Doctor David up the hill at Killcare who runs his surgery from a lop-sided cottage with sandy bird-of-paradise bushes in the garden.

When we first chose the Bay, the absence of big stores was one of the attractions. The scale of our ecosystem of shops is just right. If we need anything from the pharmacy in Umina or Woy Woy or have some dry-cleaning to send out, the shops act as depots. Radford's Pharmacy in Umina used to run a rather famous amphibious car which did the run across to the Bay by the most direct route, emerging wet and whale-like from the water to deliver orders, usually with chemist Rod Radford at the wheel.

Supermarket shopping is done at Woolworths in Woy Woy, as well equipped as any city equivalent, and Erina Fair boasts most of the big-name stores. The first time I parked right outside its branch of Grace Bros, in a level parking area the size of a modest field, I almost cried. Weeks earlier, before the move, I'd spent an hour trapped in a multi-storey carpark at Sydney's Bondi Junction trying to get to a department store. Whenever I feel nostalgic for Sydney's cafe culture and the buzz of my favourite shopping thoroughfares—Oxford, Norton, King and Bay—I remind myself how much circling I used to do, like a prowling shark, looking for somewhere to park. And how often I'd drive home, defeated.

The Bay also has its share of home-workers, rigged up by technology to offices elsewhere, and practitioners of all sorts. Tarot-card reading, feng shui, aromatherapy massage, chakra balancing: you name the New Age practice and it's on offer at the Bay. A leaflet in Thistle Do's letter-box invited us to make our own shamanic drums and Native American healing rattles (BYO feathers). We wondered if Scruffy's always ragged appearance had anything to do with him being plucked by parish rattle-makers. He often gave us the sort of haunted look that suggested he'd seen things beyond a bird's natural expectations.

The resident naturopath is David Legge, brother to Kate, a work colleague of mine. When I first mentioned to Graeme that Kate Legge's brother was a Hardys Bay naturopath, he was only half-listening. Moments later, he stared at me in a confused way and asked, 'Is there much call for that sort of thing?'

I assured Graeme that David Legge was very busy indeed and that as a matter of fact he practised in Woy Woy, too. It was much later that night when the topic came up again. 'Who'd have thought Kate Legge would have a brother who's an acrobat,' said Graeme, as he snapped off the bedside light.

•

'What do you do up there?' our Sydney friends still ask.

Free of the need to dash, we spend a lot of time breathing the air, deeply and slowly. That intrinsic Australian smell of 'eucalyptus and salty sunlight' was how novelist Sumner Locke Elliott put it. Then there's just plain old looking. The Bay cools and cleanses our eyes, its textures change according to the weather and the time of day.

When it's raining, everything shimmers in degrees of slate, like a Chinese brush-and-ink painting. 'Soft weather' is how the Irish would describe it. They're not a race to freely admit to rain. When a friend of mine took me to see the grave of William Butler Yeats in County Sligo, there was an almighty downpour of the sort that could maim birds and fell small children but as we huddled under an umbrella, he took my hand and whispered, irresistibly, 'That'll just be the angels crying at the beauty of this day.'

In the lunch-drugged continental manner, we take siestas—'the hour for daydreams', as Graham Greene declared, even if Noel Coward suggested such daytime napping was best left to 'Hindus and Argentines'. On warm evenings, we may drive to 'Cinema under the Stars' at the Avoca Beach Theatre to sit alfresco in a seaside garden ('Bring a blanket! Picnics welcome!') as the moving pictures flicker on a giant, bug-flecked screen in the soupy air of high summer. We eat before we buy our tickets, always fish and chips with sinful amounts of salt scoffed straight from the waxy paper. But once installed, we're often offered picnic morsels by fellow picture-goers who pity us for our lack of provisioning and there really is something uniquely convivial about silently sharing mysterious sandwiches in the dark with strangers.

And we talk about boats. Which are not just boats, as I've discovered. They are ferries, yachts, tinnies, rowboats, kayaks and the occasional cabin cruiser that would rate as a stretch limousine if it were on the road. Sitting on the jetty with the fishermen and sailors, I have learned of 'surgeon's loops' and 'clinched three-turn half-blood knots' and other mysterious salty things that smack of clans to which women are not easily admitted. I have discovered that New South Wales Fisheries decrees great white and grey nurse sharks are protected species which 'must be carefully returned to the water'. I like that word 'carefully' and am grateful for such solicitous instructions.

On winter mornings at the Bay, images appear from the mist like photographs being developed. On a clear, cold night, the sky seems to stretch to infinity, with an embroidery of silver stars looping and twisting like enormous amusement rides. If we stand at the end of the jetty, the navigating lights on the Pretty Beach Channel flash red, green, red, green. On New Year's Eve, we dangled our feet in the water, drank vintage French champers and lit sparklers at the jetty's end. It felt lonely but comforting, too, like a scene from *The Great Gatsby*, with Jay watching for the green light at the end of Daisy's dock.

Many Bay weekenders are trellised with tinsel and Christmas lights in season but very often the coloured globes are left up all year, threaded around decks, doors and eaves. Rarely are they turned on unless it's the proper festive season but they do have purposes other than decoration. One fisherman who likes to spend the early evenings with his line dangling at the end of Thistle Do's jetty can be seen suddenly packing up and dashing back to his truck when a rope of Christmas lights flashes on and off several times at a house across the water. We presume it's his wife signalling him home to tea. Perhaps there are other women who use the little fairy-lights as beacons to beam in their men from the Yum Yum tree when the sun is going down and the food on the table is getting cold.

Sometimes we drive down to Patonga, the less fashionable curve of coast around from Pearl Beach. Its estuarine mudflats are covered with mangroves, twisted and gnarled and looking like ghostly tramps in the dusk. The majority of fibro and timber houses on this part of the Coast appear to be held together by rubber bands, safety pins and well-placed prayers. The most celebrated of all is the twin-roofed Klein's Kabin on Patonga Creek, built by William Klein in 1924 as a fishing shack; timber was rowed across from Brooklyn and Klein hand-carried rocks for the foundations. His descendants still use the shack today and it leapt to fame when featured in the ABC-TV series based on Robert Drewe's 'The Bodysurfers'.

Patonga locals talk of 'the dark corner' where residents held out against new-bothered electricity for as long as it could. The Pittwater-facing mansions of Palm Beach across the water could as well be rooted on another planet.

The Patonga–Palm Beach ferry, small and wooden, makes daily crossings to Planet Pittwater, past Lion Island with its shape of a feline *couchant*. One summer morning we travelled across to visit Ken and Jane from Sydney at their grand weekender and, for the first time since the move north, looked back at our section of the thickly forested Coast, pointing out to our friends the jutting bulk of Box Head and the wild shoreline of Putty Beach. So near in avian terms that I knew exactly how Harry Pickett must have felt as he tried to soar off the barn roof with his wings of canvas and pasted feathers.

It was with some reluctance that I stayed landbound, at least until we reboarded the ferry to bob back to Patonga.

Holiday Home Survival Kit

What a renter gets in a holiday house is someone else's idea of decor. And that can mean shagpile carpet and orange benchtops. If you suspect the decor could give you a headache, pack calico or cotton throws (cheap Indian bedspreads are ideal) to disguise hideous lounge chairs and sofas, splash out on flowers and take your brightest towels, cushions and tablecloths and favourite bed-linen.

Don't presume the obligatory Scrabble set and jumbo jigsaw will have all their own pieces. A BYO beach-house survival kit should include playing cards, at least one board game and an unopened jigsaw (as surety against missing bits). If the house doesn't have a VCR, enquire through the letting agent about hiring one via a local store and, if possible, have it wired up before you arrive. This is an essential wet-weather back-up if you are travelling with children.

If it's a house with just one television set, it may pay to take along a portable so adults and children can watch separately.

Depending on space available in the car, a few folding director's chairs can jazz up a terrace. Always ask the agent to confirm that the barbecue is in good working order as beach living is all about outdoor eating. As my mother always said, 'There's no holiday in cooking.' And she always insisted on a torch, which may sound Boy Scoutish but, if you arrive at night and the agent has left the key 'under the mat' (with the spiders), you'll be very glad to be so prepared.

CHAPTER EIGHT

The Summer People

'So the season opens and the usual crowd fling into their estate wagons bags and dogs and cats and children and potties and swimsuits and tennis rackets and sleeping bags and hamsters. And take off as they always do at this time of the year for the coast.'

from *Summer People* by Janice Elliott

Once I had been one of the Summer People, holidaying with my parents at a series of seaside enclaves along the New South Wales coast. Mollymook, Budgewoi, Terrigal: all names intrinsically associated with sun, sea and sedation. Graeme had written an evocative piece for a newspaper about his Christmas holidays at Sorrento on Melbourne's Port Phillip Bay and he read it aloud to me as the first waves of Summer People arrived at the Bay.

He had written of Sorrento as 'a magical, barefoot, short-sleeved place'. He stayed with his Grandma and

Old Pop Stanger, in their little place halfway between the Front Beach and the unruly Back Beach. There were 'beached stingrays and bleached cuttlefish shells on sand banks'. Young Graeme would walk on the rocks when the tide went out, stepping over holes so deep and mysterious that if you fell in, you'd likely end up in China.

Some nights, they'd all go down to the Back Beach and light a driftwood fire to cook periwinkles. 'Grandma would have baked bread and boiled some eggs,' he read to me. 'Other nights, Old Pop Stanger and Dad would disappear, wrapped up in woolly jumpers and oilskins. Hours later, they'd return with buckets of crayfish and tip them out on to the floor of the back verandah. Grabbing a cavalryman's sabre, Pop'd chase those scurrying crays as if the Last Charge had just been sounded.'

He'd called that piece 'The Summer of Fifty-Five' but in fact he'd written of many summers rolled into one. I realised my childhood was like that, too. Memory has a sly way of telescoping time and when I look back, it has all become one long, hot day, with sand between my toes and ice cream all sticky on my fingers.

As we discussed those times in a more philosophical way than we had when buying Peacock Cottage and making the move, we both realised we'd been searching for innocence and optimism. Having veered off from our childhoods in busy, often exotic directions, he to the world of the theatre and me to a life of travel, we had returned, tired and replete, to an approximation of where it began, to a time of wonder and possibility. Just as we both knew this relationship would be the last and the most important for each of us, we realised the Bay was our final port of call. No melancholy in that revelation. It simply felt good to be home.

•

Thus resolved, Graeme and I could assume the smug posture of insiders, viewing the newcomers as a highly coloured migratory species possessed of peculiar habits. As soon as the private schools broke up, a day or so prior to their public counterparts, conga lines of space wagons and smart four-wheel-drives would start to arrive, hurtling down Killcare Road at an impatient pace that fairly shrieked holidaymaker. Mother Mary told us most of the summer flock were from Sydney's leafy north shore or the garden belt of Eastwood and beyond. Families from the toney eastern suburbs preferred the Palm Beach peninsula, which was closer. From the north side of Sydney, the Bay can be reached in about an hour. We read a statistic on Thistle Do's deck one morning that some 85 per cent of Australians live less than 50 kilometres from the sea. No wonder we all rush to the coast come holiday time, like eager lemmings.

Hardys Bay was 'easy-access Eden' according to one real estate advertising writer. Maybe too easy, we were beginning to fear.

The Bay's status as a self-contained community, not en route to anywhere else, has enormous appeal, much like 'SeaChange''s Pearl Bay, cut off from the world by a collapsed bridge. When a big tourist sign sprang up on Empire Bay Drive announcing a distance of less than half a kilometre to our importantly capitalised Scenic Region, we knew we'd been marked as what the Brits are fond of calling a Beauty Spot.

In summer there's a real buzz, and it's not an entirely unpleasant undercurrent. All around are vignettes that defy categorising into any particular decade. Kids fishing off the jetty or mucking around at low tide, families making veritable stockades on the sand at Putty Beach with their umbrellas and Eskys and folding chairs. Corporate men strutting with expense-account paunches, their too-small cossies bunched in front like windsocks. The sort of men who look as if they'd smoke cigars in the bath and whose enhanced hairlines, when wet, take on the appearance of failed crops. I kept searching for one in 'a straw hat with a red band and a brief pair of leopard print trunks' like Kevin Parnell, the World Famous Suntan Champion in the Robert Drewe short story, 'The Silver Medallist'. 'Skin like cracked vinyl,' said Graeme of the serious sunbakers. Given my childhood experiences with Mother's coconut oil, it's a wonder I have not turned reptilian, too.

But with the summer throngs came 'moments', as Graeme calls them. Pipi gathering, for instance, reached an all-time high. The New South Wales Fisheries Department decrees that these little molluscs must only be collected for bait, and certainly no more than 50 per person at one time. But they're good eating for humans, too, and the sand along the Coast was being torn up by hundreds of summer gatherers. We read of a man who was to be fined for digging up more than 2000 pipis from Birubi Beach, north of Newcastle.

The temperatures rose, tempers flared. And then there were the Summer Dogs. When Summer People travel, their pets—or 'companion animals' as the sticklers for political correctness would have it—go too. A pampered pooch would likely need counselling if it were to be left in boarding kennels rather than included in a family holiday. But many city dogs do not easily make the transition to the seaside, a fact that has escaped the attention of some owners.

It's lovely to see a dog who's rarely let off the lead run free: ears flapping, tail wagging, legs going for all they're worth. It's less enjoyable when it's chasing native birds or bounding down a pier with such purpose that fishermen have to hurriedly jump out of its trajectory.

Where there's canine there's urine, and worse. Which presents another problem at the Bay where front fences are rare and gardens lovingly tended. Locals walk their dogs with plastic bags, as is the well-mannered way, to neatly dispose of any droppings. But some Summer People, overcome by fresh air and the proximity of so much bushland, take no such polite precautions, fondly imagining, no doubt, that they are in a totally organic environment.

Even those who've rented cottages with a no-pets rule somehow sneak them in. 'What dog?' they protest to the real estate agent who, alerted by neighbours, pays a surprise visit. How about that dog over there, the one with a peacock feather in its mouth? Alfredo left home in a huff. Chased from the garden by assorted hounds, he did one last promenade of the deck, screeching like a soprano on opening night, his splendid tail spread full-circle. Then he stuck his little beak in the air and flew up the hill in the direction of the Bouddi National Park.

If you've never seen an airborne peacock, it's a sight both awesome and alarming, like watching a very fat person perform a pirouette. Even the kookaburras stopped mid-cackle as Alfredo sailed off in the style of a Catalina flying boat with a glorious blue underbelly.

Down on the shores of the Bay, Charles and Camilla went into hiding among the old-man mangroves. Just as the sun was setting and the dogs were back in their summer gardens, the ducks could be coaxed out with pieces of bread torn from a brown loaf.

But next morning the Summer Dogs would be at it again and we began to recognise their distinctive barks and the reason for their excitement. Things got very yappy if they found a cat to harass—most of the local moggies have lost their youthful figures and make non-sporting prey—or a pelican to chase or a flock of feeding galahs to terrorise. Absolute hysteria if they got a brush turkey in their sights. But these Bay birds are given to kick boxing and I found myself putting a little bandage on a docile bitser's leg, simultaneously patting his head and cursing his owner. My colleague Jane Fraser, listening to this tale, smartly reprimanded me for failing to keep up with dogspeak. There's no such thing as a bitser or a mongrel any more, she warned. 'Random breed', if I didn't mind.

One January Sunday, a Labrador came trotting into Thistle Do's garden looking for a scratching post. He had around his neck one of those collars, like an inverted lampshade, that vets rig up after treatments to stop dogs scratching their faces. He looked like a clown in a ruff and as his owner appeared to pile him into a loaded jeep, I went in search of Alfredo to tell him it was time to come home. The circus was leaving town.

•

It's a bit of a tradition for the locals to throw an end-of-summer party under the Yum Yum tree, the advent of cooler weather heralding a return to sleepy-hollow normality. 'A party like this couldn't happen anywhere else in the world,' said one of our favourite tradies, cradling a tinnie. 'Except Mexico, of course,' said another. After a few moments of contemplative silence and shuffling, someone else cracked open a can and said, 'Well, that'd be right. Here's to bloody Mexico, then.' An unlikely toast to the land of siestas and sombreros from its amigos under the Yum Yum tree.

The season was at its official end but the weather was defying all notion of autumn. So the Summer People came at Easter, too, amid rich sunshine and swimmable seas. It was a time to think of bunnies—and of hares and tortoises. And of road accident tolls and bad driving habits, especially where the lead-footed lapin was concerned. Holidays always go too fast and perhaps that's why motoring hares feel compelled to drive like mad, to be at their destination quick and early, if not dead on time. Road rage has become a catchphrase but it has been around ever since the car that could overtake a Model T Ford was manufactured. The very progress of traffic is like a race, a great exercise in weaving and dodging, albeit with no line honours or prizes, save for the smug satisfaction of getting there first.

Given the number of times Graeme and I have commuted along the F3 Motorway, we've dubbed ourselves Bay City Rollers. And we've become experts on the driving habits of holiday hares and tortoises. Not that the latter are too much trouble, except when leaving the motorway on the Coast-bound journey and getting stuck behind one inching its way uphill to the peninsula on the curving single-lane stretch. Huff, puff, grunt, grind. I would turn up the CD player and practise deep-breathing exercises so I'd be calm next time I called Telstra or an airline frequent-flyer booking hotline to be put on hold with Enya for an hour.

Invariably, behind me would be a hare, so close I could look into my rear-view mirror and count nostril hairs. Almost touching my back bumper, it'd be as if the hare was about to convert to a front-end loader and scoop me and the tortoise out of the way. Often the pressure got too much in these situations where I was the driver caught as the stuffing in the tortoise-and-hare combo and I'd do a dangerous overtake to get out of the gridlock.

It's road intimidation at its worst, but sadly such lack of road etiquette continues to be a feature of the Bay and adjacent Coast during any holiday period. The security railings on the steep Wards Hill Road corners regularly are dented; the speed signs say 15 kilometres per hour but motorists new to the road ignore this limit and go careering around, often taking the bends way too widely. One morning as Graeme drove me to Woy Woy Station to catch the train to the city, we saw a kombi van hanging off the edge with two large men holding its back bumper so it wouldn't fall down. They were from a second vehicle; the kombi people were still in the front seat of their van waiting for the police and ambulance to arrive. We haven't seen any other incidents in such detail but the railings still sprout new gouges and dents.

Certain trees on Wards Hill Road are used as message boards, announcing babies and birthdays, garage sales and greetings. 'Clair's Corner: She's Back' recently appeared on a fence around a bend on Killcare Road. Adam told us that a similar message was scrawled there years ago and a local soon added, 'Who the hell is Clair?' On the F3, Jolls Bridge has had its sign personalised to Joels Bridge. Go, Joel: I don't usually approve of defacement but there's something grand and appealing about appropriating a corner or, better still, a whole bridge. The poet Henry Kendall thought so, too; he carved his initials into the wooden bed upon which he slept at the Fagan farm in Gosford where he stayed in the 1870s. Sir Henry Parkes later appointed him as Inspector of Forests; a curious role for a bard and not involving, we must presume, any defacing of trees.

Frequently I regale Graeme, the reluctant driver, with stories of motoring in foreign parts. In Asia, I've informed him, road rules exist merely as ethereal concepts. Once, in India, I asked a guide why our driver was overtaking on blind corners, running red lights and side-swiping auto-rickshaws. 'He's a Hindu. He believes in reincarnation,' was not the reply I wanted to hear. Nothing to do but trust in karma and study the road signs: 'This road is not a racetrack' or 'If married to speed, divorce her'. My letter to Gosford City Council suggesting the erection of two such signs on Wards Hill Road (plus an inspired one of my own—'Drive like a hare and get jugged') remains unanswered, no doubt relegated to the circular filing cabinet, as my sons call waste-paper bins.

In the Philippines, jeepneys, those colourfully converted American army jeeps that act as mini-buses, sport horns that blare out pop songs and the taxis toot incessantly. I asked a Manila tour guide why everyone was making such a racket. 'It is for information only,' I was told. In Japan, I once saw a road sign diverting traffic around a development site. It commanded: 'Drive sideways'. It made me instantly think of Italy where I've seen a motorist lift up one of those tiny toy cars which look as if they should have a key in the roof, place it to one side, and park his larger vehicle in the spot. Sideways! Too squeezy for the driver to get out? What else is a sunroof to be used for in Florence in January?

Travel writer Bill Bryson has advised that the only way to safely cross a busy street in Rome is to find a passing nun and stick to her like a sweaty T-shirt as the traffic only stops for holy sisters. Roberto, my guide in Naples, told me there are no pedestrians in Italy, only people trying to find where they have parked their cars.

You wouldn't think parking at the Bay would be a problem—there's never been any timed or metered zones, apart from designated bus stops and the odd No Standing notice on a narrow road—but that would scarcely stop the Summer People from charging into the Old Killcare Store and demanding instant attention because they were 'double parked'.

•

> *Jet ski person selfish fink,*
> *may your silly jet ski sink.*
> *May you hit a pile of rocks,*
> *oh hoonish summer coastal pox.*
> Michael Leunig

From the deck of Thistle Do, there is a near-180 degree vista of water, looking across to Pretty Beach and Wagstaffe at one angle, and further along to the Rip Bridge, Booker Bay and the Ettalong flats. A dirt road between the wild rosemary bush hedge and the fishing jetty became almost like a race track in summer. A turning circle just beyond the house turned into the equivalent of a suburban roundabout. Our heads swivelled like tennis umpires as we sat in old cane chairs and tried to keep up with all the activity. Jet skis were the most obvious intrusion, waking us early and continuing through the day, disturbing the Outer during games of cricket on the sandbars at low tide.

Not that we could complain about the amount of traffic cruising past Thistle Do: we were lively sightseers ourselves, motoring around the Coast's smaller bays and inlets, taking photos and making notes.

To make the research for this book easier, I carried a tape recorder and spoke into it as I drove. One afternoon as I meandered through Phegans Bay, up and around its bendy roads, photographing cottages with straggle-toothed fences and veiled with morning glory vines, I stopped to peer at a sign stuck to a telegraph pole. I got out of the car and read into the tape recorder: 'Lost goat. Reward'. A man appeared at my elbow, looked all around to ensure we were alone and whispered, 'Would you be from one of those current affairs shows?'

Perhaps there is still a scoop to be had concerning the goat snatchers of Phegans Bay. It would make a good plot for an episode of 'SeaChange', at least. With the series being repeated by ABC-TV, new episodes on the way and the beach-house interior design wave not yet abated, more and more of our friends were talking of a change of scene. Some of them have actually done it on a permanent basis: Charles and Helen to Mollymook on the New South Wales South Coast, Moya and Ross and Shirley to Kangaroo Valley south of Sydney, Christine and Melvin to South Australia. Alison and Ken have a shed for weekends in the Hunter Valley;

other mates have bought at Avoca, Patonga and Pearl Beach. All spurred on by a need to flee the city and return to basics, with the millennium looming as the mother of all watersheds.

Design magazines went coastal that summer in their full-gloss spreads, profiling beach houses so deeply glamorous it's hard to imagine anyone using them solely as weekenders. Terms such as spatial planning, minimal impact, cantilevering and pavilion roofs were creeping into the copy. Glass walls and witty corrugated iron dividers ruled. The interiors looked cold and remote, as if they'd been decorated by caterers: all stainless steel, with the odd piece of perfectly proportioned fruit standing to attention.

The *Sydney Morning Herald*'s 'Domain' lift-out surprised regular readers by spreading beyond the suburban norm to Mackerel Beach on Pittwater, accessed by ferry from Palm Beach. We read of locals scooting about in tinnies in this 'small, isolated haven', of a carefree community culture of 'old shorts and bare feet' and ranch-style homes built on goat tracks. 'Heaven,' we chorused that Thursday morning, as we imagined a place with no road, just as it was at the Bay when miserly old Hardy served his plonk under that earliest of Yum Yum trees and tipsy boaties rowed home.

But it wasn't just the design writers and real estate journalists who had coastal fever. Australia's best-known authors were at it, too. Tim Winton came up with a short story about Christmas holidays in a shack 'with a big, windblown veranda' at the mouth of the Greenough River, just south of Geraldton in Western Australia. 'The most remarkable place to have year after year,' he mused, 'and I sometimes think that it was this house that caused me to become a writer.

'Out the back was a water tank, high on a rough jarrah stand, and sheds that contained the generator and the bucket shower I came to dread. Further along was the thunderbox dunny, a place of mystery and fascination, and a sort of half-open greenhouse crammed with cactus. From the front windows you could see out beyond the eyelid of the veranda to the bright limestone road and the river mouth... The house itself consisted mainly of one huge L-shaped room lined with beds, remnants of other houses and times and places.'

It reminded me of Paul Dyer's description of his Ettalong holidays, lined up with his brother and sister in hard and uncomfortable single beds, talking and giggling into the night. 'After the lights went out, I'd be aware of the sound of the fridge,' he said. 'It was a rickety old thing, with the freezer below—we'd have to go every other day to the petrol station and buy a block of ice for it—and it would shake and twitch all night.'

•

Summer means cricket so Graeme and I stayed at the Surry Hills apartment for days at a time to attend matches at the Sydney Cricket Ground and to catch up with city friends. Joe was off travelling again and the little apartment seemed forlorn without a permanent resident.

Eduardo and Alex had painted it according to my choice of very bold colours—as hot and wild as Peacock Cottage was cool and pastel. The combined lounge and dining rooms were burgundy red, the main bedroom a sunflower-yellow, the second bedroom a Granny Smith green and the two bathroom ceilings were hyacinth and magenta. With its parquetry floor and wooden blinds it looked positively tropical, and every time Graeme and I were there for more than a few days we spruced it up and aired the rooms and tried to make it feel more homely.

It was set on a busy street, and we found the readjustment to city noise very difficult. At first, we'd found the Bay too quiet; we'd lie in bed straining our ears for any kind of sound. When something did make a noise, like a twig falling on Thistle Do's roof, our eyes would snap open. In Surry Hills, there were ambulances and police sirens and early-morning trucks, all seemingly loud enough to be in the bedroom with us.

But the building itself—a converted warehouse with industrial windows and thick walls—was quiet. We could hear people walking along the hallway but no sounds came from neighbouring apartments. 'People upstairs all practise ballet...their living room is a bowling alley,' wrote Ogden Nash of apartment living. Maybe we were just lucky in our positioning, but disturbances were few. Our radio friend Bruce knew Kevin, who lived in an opposite apartment, and he'd told us to listen for his bagpipes. We had visions of Kevin the urban piper playing grimly, striving to be heard above the din of the traffic, but sadly no sounds ever wafted our way.

I'd never lived in an apartment before but had been conscious of a residential stigma attached to living in a high-rise rather than proving one's success by fulfilling the Great Australian Dream of a proper home of one's own. I remember a new girl joining my Year 10 class in the late 1960s and her being introduced as someone who lived in a flat. The school being a sheltered middle-class ladies college full of doctors' daughters, we all gasped. How bohemian, we thought, imagining a flat as a sort of bedsit where strangers made love on beanbags and no one ever emptied the ashtrays.

In the early 1970s, when the television soap 'Number 96' was as madly popular as 'Neighbours' and the like are today, the shenanigans of those who lived in that block of flats confirmed our beliefs of decadence. Live in a flat, I decided, and the next thing you'd know, a bare-breasted Abigail would be banging on your door asking to borrow not so much a cup of sugar as a condom and a tube of KY jelly.

Some time in the late 1970s, flats became units, and then apartments, which sounded so sophisticated, so New York and bachelorish. To be an apartment dweller smacked of cosmopolitan delights—skyline views, Hugh Hefner–style dressing gowns, crafty mirrored walls, patios where one served cocktails at sunset, perhaps toasting the happy absence of lawn-mowers and leaves in the guttering.

In pre-Olympics Sydney, blocks of apartments were shooting up with sluttish abandon. Many of the buildings appeared to have nothing in their favour, aside from a lifetime's work for window-cleaning contractors. Cranes dotted the skyline, main-street lanes were closed for construction works, traffic jammed in complicated octopus-like coils, and road rage and muggings were out of control. As the summer rain fell in sheets and the city glistened dark and menacing, like a Ridley Scott film-set, we fled back to the Bay.

CHAPTER NINE

Hooray for Hardywood

The tall white sails emerge above the bay's
Low and level veils of morning haze.

Haiku by Nakao Gakoku, translated by Harold Stewart

The Japanese haiku poet Nakao Gakoku worked in the 17th century so we know *he* didn't set foot in our Bay, but as the year drifted on we realised that what we considered to be a secret hideaway was well known to a broad cross-section of our friends. Celebrities, major and minor, of the sort not attracted by notice-me beaches of the Palm and Pearl ilk, holiday at the Bay, many at houses they bought years ago and use for just a few weeks each summer.

We discovered that Peacock Cottage is just a few doors from a holiday house owned by writers Robert Drewe and Candida Baker. Theirs is reached by 87 steps and sits in magisterial aloofness, amid spotted gums and angophoras, atop a ridge with a pulpit's view of Pretty Beach and the Bay. Robert has written extensively about the Australian coast and, given his druthers, would live permanently at the Bay, walking his dog, Ella, and tinkering with short stories. Candida and I both work at the *Australian* and in the first months after our move we'd often compare notes about who'd spent more whole days at the Bay that month. I always won, as the school needs of Robert's and Candida's young son, Sam, kept them 'in town'.

According to Candida, the Bay has something the Palms and the Pearls of this world don't have—'a touch of wilderness, and therefore wildness, which takes it out of the rather claustrophobic confines of its semi-precious neighbours'.

Actor and theatre director John Bell of the Bell Shakespeare Company and his actor wife, Anna Volska, have bought a substantial house at Wagstaffe among mint-green gardens which are in a robust state of continual planting and tending by Adam. We spoke briefly to John after the premiere of his company's production of 'The Tempest' at the Sydney Opera House. 'Your gardens are looking marvellous,' he said in his wonderfully resonant voice before sweeping off to find himself a drink. Graeme and I were confused: we had no garden at Surry Hills and it seemed inconceivable that the fame of the Hanging Gardens of the Bay had spread to inner Shakespearean circles. Anna sought us out to tell us about their Wagstaffe connection and to explain that

Adam had pointed out Graeme's terraces one day. We all drank a toast to the Bay, John with traces of Prospero's makeup melting into his collar.

One Saturday morning as Graeme was buying newspapers at the general store, he bumped into actor Greg Pickhaver, better known as H.G. Nelson of Club Buggery fame. They were old friends from Graeme's Melbourne theatre days. Greg had recently bought some land at the Bay and had his architect in tow. Moments later, in walked playwright Katherine Thomson who did a double-take at the sight of Graeme. The day before, she'd been in Sydney attending rehearsals of her play, 'Navigating', in which Graeme was playing Ian Donnelly ('clean, smooth—in that small-town sort of way', according to the script notes). Neither one realised the other had a real-life small-town connection.

Actor Bruce Spence and his wife, Jenny, are building on a hinterland acreage behind MacMasters Beach. Film director Ray Lawrence is up on the heights. Actors Wendy Hughes, Judy Morris and Penny Cook became familiar sights through summer; friends of Graeme's from Sydney advertising and film production waved to him on weekends. SBS television executive Nigel Milan had built a two-storey white and lavender rippled-tin and concrete edifice on the heights; it has won an architectural award for beach-house architecture but locals still mock it as the Fridge or the Esky.

People Graeme hadn't seen in years were suddenly standing next to him buying newspapers. We bumped into the well-known literary agent Tim Curnow at Skippers Seafood in Umina one evening and he advised us what sort of fish to order with our chips. He was holidaying with his kids in a caravan, happily and simply, as they'd always done.

We spent a night at Headlands, a minuscule retreat of two bungalows and a pair of bush-facing rooms set high above Pretty Beach. The bungalows have private plunge pools and spas and decks which jut into the trees. All very next-to-nature, including kookaburras dive-bombing the outdoors breakfast table and Eric the eastern water dragon wandering in to help himself to any stray insects and, if he's in the mood, to take a cooling dip. But as he sometimes gets stuck in the pool, it's suggested to guests they dangle a towel into the water so he can haul himself out.

I'd met owners Garry and Greg before but hadn't realised there was another connection. In previous incarnations, before the magnetic pull of the Bay took hold, Garry had played piano in one of Graeme's Melbourne theatre productions. It was to Headlands that actor Judy Nunn and her husband, Bruce Venables, were bound when they first visited the Bay in 1991. Gobsmacked by the scenery, they ran into the car in front and had to be towed up the steep drive to Headlands. Very soon afterwards, they bought a place down by the water. Garry and Greg report that other Headlands guests have been similarly smitten by the palliative powers of the Bay, turning property-owners in the blink of an eye, much to the delight of Mother Mary who jokes about paying spotter fees.

Another of our Bay mini-escapes was north to Toowoon Bay, between Bateau Bay and The Entrance, where Kims Resort has been operating for more than a century, run by four generations of the Strachan family. Originally, it was Kims Camp, a bare-basics fishing getaway, and it still has the air of enclave with its century-old Norfolk pines, timber bungalows angled toward the water, those in dress-circle position with lofty views, and some with spas or micro-pools on their wood-planked decks.

There are peacocks and their paramour hens roaming the estate and usually a celebrity or two in residence, hiding behind dark glasses. Three times a day, a brass bell with a sea-faring tone summons the idle to meals— a throwback to the time when gentlemen wore pocket watches, but never at the beach.

The current owner, Andrew Strachan, remembers Toowoon Bay as 'all dirt and sand and wildness and freedom' when he arrived with his parents in the 1950s from the greenery of Katoomba in the Blue Mountains. 'There were at least seven poultry and citrus farms along The Entrance road at that time,' he told me. Now, just one remains, where supplies are still purchased for dishes that make up Kims legendary buffet spreads. Seville oranges were sold at roadside stalls around Kincumber in the early days, and Andrew's late grandmother used to make Kims marmalade from this beautifully bitter fruit. Luckily, the family recipe has been passed on, although the Sevilles are no longer available in such ample profusion.

Toowoon Bay was settled in 1829 and was first known as Chinaman's Bay because of the number of Chinese fishermen who set up camps along the shore. Canton Beach on Tuggerah Lake, just south of Toukley, was another popular spot for the Chinese, and those associations live on in its name. Mullet, blackfish, bream, abalone and schnapper were caught and cured and sent as far afield as China. Meanwhile, the Chinese were also industrious on the Palm Beach peninsula. A fish drying business run by one Ah Chuey was particularly prosperous and he marketed his goods to Melbourne's large Chinese population.

Graeme and I had discussed these fishy connections on our initial visit to Kims in 1995. It was our first weekend away together and we were both a little nervous. I wasn't amused when I went to pick him up for the drive to Toowoon Bay and found he was travelling with a stash of 16 books. He seemed to think it was perfectly normal to be so equipped but I took it as being his back-up measure against a potentially boring weekend.

Later, he explained that he was halfway through reading them for a composite crime review he was preparing for the *Australian*. He still manages to read about six books at once, leaving them around the house and picking one up as he passes for a quick half-page on his way to, say, the kitchen. I can only keep track of one book at a time and had packed just a collection of romantic short stories for Kims, hoping Graeme and I might star in some Mills and Boon–worthy scenarios of our own.

The weekend went well, particularly when Graeme discovered I love cricket and was perfectly happy lounging about watching a game on television. But when we did go for a walk along the beach, I realised Graeme's notion of beachwear was black cowboy boots, black jeans and black T-shirt. Forever the urban animal, it had been years and years since he'd had a weekend in the country. Despite the temperatures being in the low thirties, he had even slung in his black leather jacket.

As we were waiting to check out of Kims, we noticed a gallery of fine Max Dupain photographs on the wall of the reception foyer. We both looked for a long time at one showing about a dozen people wading through water, some carrying buckets, all looking intently downwards. The caption read 'Prawning at Toowoon Bay'. I realised, in horror, that Graeme had tears in his eyes. 'It's so sad,' he whispered. This was a man who had demolished a seafood platter for dinner the previous evening with no sign of unease. 'I wonder if they ever found the body?' he added, wandering outside for some fresh air. I looked again at Dupain's handwriting. Graeme had read 'Drowning at Toowoon Bay'.

Such malapropisms were to become common in the early days of our relationship. Graeme had admired the Japanese bathrobes at Kims with their loose sleeves and geometric navy-and-white patterns. I rang the managers Diana and Peter and arranged to buy one for Graeme as a Christmas present. It duly arrived and on Christmas Day as we had lunch with Justin and Joe, Graeme informed them I had given him a yakuza. Now, that's the Japanese word for an underworld gangster but I guess it's not oceans away from yukata, the word for a loose dressing gown.

Justin and Joe both speak Japanese, and so the wind-up began. 'Where did Mum find the present?' asked Justin.

'At Toowoon Bay,' replied Graeme.

'Where exactly?' continued Joe.

'Well, rolled up at the end of the bed, initially,' said Graeme, who had no idea where the conversation was going, 'but then your mother went to the reception desk to see if they had another one the same for sale. But they didn't, so they ordered one for her.'

'And where will you keep the yakuza?' enquired Justin.

'Behind the bathroom door!' exclaimed Graeme, who was getting fed up with what he took to be Justin's pedantry.

By this time, Justin, Joe and I were falling about. Luckily, Graeme is incredibly good-natured and enjoys a joke at his own expense. So now we always use the word yakuza instead of yukata, and vice-versa, which astonished some film-world friends of Graeme when he was talking about director Ridley Scott's work during a shoot and mentioned that his favourite was *Black Rain*, the one where all those yukatas are running around Osaka.

•

New neighbours moved in next to us at Thistle Do. 'At least this won't be anyone we know,' laughed Graeme as he poured the evening shandies. An hour later, Chris came to the door to introduce himself. Which wasn't really necessary. It was Chris Pate, son of veteran actor Michael. Graeme didn't know Chris well but they'd met in the past when his mother, Philippa, was Graeme's agent in Melbourne.

As is often the way, the more famous the visitor, the more downbeat the clothing and car. An American actor who stayed with us for a few days in January managed to escape detection by simply not wearing makeup. She took rolls and rolls of film and kept saying things like, 'It's just as weird as that show "Northern Exposure" on television, but there's no snow.' We think of our life at the Bay more as a cross between 'The Good Life' and 'Green Acres', with Susan wearing lace gloves to pick spiders out of Graeme's hair and painting a watercolour of the one organic tomato we've managed so far in Peacock Cottage's veggie patch.

Up behind Thistle Do, on a ridge shaggy with trees, live the two Pauls of the Old Killcare Store, refugees from Sydney's Surry Hills, who looked high, low, far and near for their ultimate 'haven'. One wanted ocean and the other mountains, and they'd all but given up finding anywhere that successfully combined the two. 'We were invited to a birthday party at Umina,' Paul Booth told me, 'and not knowing where it was or how long it would take, on the designated day we set off from Sydney for the Central Coast at 9 a.m. for a 4 p.m. invitation.

'We arrived at out motel at 11 a.m. and, tearing ourselves away from the beautiful exposed-brick decor of our room, we picked up a map and set off to explore.

We drove across the Rip Bridge, headed for Kincumber and Terrigal and as we went along Empire Bay Drive, I looked at the map and suggested we turned right to Wagstaffe.'

Almost missing the turn and then arguing over further directions, the two Pauls arrived at Hardys Bay and each wandered in a different direction 'in separate and equal obstinacy'. Until they met back at the car and cried, in unison, 'This is it!'

'This place has everything,' Paul Booth tells me. 'There's ocean, a quiet bay village atmosphere and beautiful hills which give the feeling of being in the mountains.' Just like Graeme and I did, the Pauls bought a rundown home that day, the deal sealed by the presence of Charles and Camilla waddling, in their usual proprietorial way, along the road.

'None of our friends had ever heard of the place and thought we were quite mad,' adds Paul Arrowsmith. 'A quite famous resident was the first person we met after we moved in and when we told him how we'd happened upon the Bay, he responded that most people find it by accident but they never leave.'

The Pauls, with their easy laughter that lassos you in, and year-round roster of house-guests, remain one of our best sources of Bay intelligence—and gossip, naturally.

•

The Bay may be edging toward trendiness but it is nothing like such famous escape hatches as the Hamptons, with their weekend chateaux and overpopulated lawns to rival those of Jay Gatsby. Apparently, it can take three or four hours to drive 130 kilometres east from New York to the exclusive beach towns of Southampton, Bridgehampton and East Hampton. James Langton, writing in the *Good Weekend* magazine insert in the *Sydney Morning Herald* and the *Age*, quoted one Manhattan businesswoman as saying, 'It's like every bad aspect of New York gets transplanted to the Hamptons for the weekend. Why would a person drive three to four hours through burnt pines and bland highways just to be with a bunch of cigar-chomping comb-overs with vanity plates on their Porsches?'

Quite.

•

An early celebrity settler of the region was the poet Henry Kendall, who spent two years living with Peter and Margaret Fagan in their home on Coorumbene Creek, Gosford, where an adjoining orchard was so heavy with oranges that visitors could pay a sixpenny toll and gorge their fill. The dwelling had been the Red Cow Inn until around 1868. Kendall arrived in Gosford in late 1873 in bad health but he was able to help on the Fagan selection, his constitution slowly improved and he wrote a body of verse about the Coast. His first child, Araluen, died just after her first birthday—'to tread another shore' he wrote in the poem dedicated to her. Araluen Drive is the main street of the Bay today, looping around the foreshore, every home with a view of the sort to inspire poetry.

The squat stone building, now known as Kendall Cottage, functions as the headquarters of the Brisbane Water Historical Society, where Elaine Fry and her energetic team guard the poet's legacy and distribute a wealth of information about the Coast's history and heritage. The colonial sofa which served as the poet's bed takes pride of place in the cottage-museum; the setting is of an oasis, hemmed in by a light industrial estate, supermarket and identikit townhouses. 'If you walk down a gentle slope from Kendall Cottage,' the Kendall Cottage Trust booklet advises, 'you will come to a spot where a grove of she-oaks and other native trees conceal a small watercourse...It is hard to believe that once ships anchored here and sent their crews up to seek shelter and company at the inn which stood near by.'

The grandly named Henry Robert Cox II—he was the Woy Woy man who named his house Kirei after travels in Japan—was a patron of the theatre and entertained on an extravagant scale, bringing up groups of actors from Sydney for parasoled parties in his garden and well-catered fishing picnics. The great French actress Sarah Bernhardt was one such visitor in 1891, and Cox had a rough bridge of planks built over the creek so she could safely cross at high tide without wetting her shoes. For some time afterwards, local fishermen referred to the makeshift walkway as the Sarah Bernhardt Bridge.

'Australia...it is so far away,' mused Bernhardt, years later, when asked by writer Katharine Susannah Pritchard what she thought of the Land Down Under. No one quite knows what she made of Woy Woy but she did have two legs at the time of her bridge crossing. She had one amputated in 1915 but continued to appear on stage, even playing the part of Napoleon's son, as I discovered while consulting the remarkable library of Maisie, widow of the artist Russell Drysdale, who was always known to family and friends as Tass.

Maisie lives on a bushy estate, once planted with beans, way up on the Bouddi heights in a long, low house designed by Guilford Bell. It's glass-walled on its ridge-facing side, with deep views down to Kincumber and Bensville, full of paintings and personal treasures and awash with the lively spirit of this wonderful woman who describes herself as 'a garrulous old lady with a stick' and laughingly says that what she most admires about the house is its complete lack of steps. The Drysdales moved to the Bay in 1965, urged by naturalist Eric Worrell to seek a *cordon sanitaire* away from Sydney.

Maisie tells me that if you look at this part of the Coast on a map, there are so many bays and inlets it appears as if mice have been nibbling the shore. A big old bird-feeding tray in her ridgetop garden, with a rather merry roof, is swarmed by 'the carnivores' as she calls them—magpies and kookaburras coming to feast at the trough.

Writers George Johnston and Charmian Clift were frequent guests of the Drysdales. Gary Kinnane, author of *George Johnston: A Biography*, writes of 'a constant stream of colourful visitors' descending upon Bouddi—'artists, writers, politicians'. John Gorton stayed at Bouddi and sat for what was to be a controversial portrait, and George Johnston holed up to write the script for an ABC television profile of Tass Drysdale. The Bouddi estate—'in the scrub', according to Geoffrey Dutton—soon became known as 'the Gosford Opera House' to those who attended the Drysdales' informal salons.

'Sit on George's stool,' ordered Maisie on my first visit, referring to Johnston's favourite perch, as I dithered over where to prop myself at her long and business-like cocktail bar. Maisie still relishes the thought of people dropping by 'who can hold conversations in words of more than two syllables', as she crisply puts it.

Maisie's theory on the perils of dropping out is a sound one. She warns that intellectual stimulation is imperative and anyone who makes a sea change to a pretty spot just because there are wonderful views and cheap real estate may regret it. 'They find there's no one to talk to and end up drinking themselves to death,' she says.

George Johnston was a follower of feng shui, which must have been a very avant-garde belief in 1968 when he penned an essay on the perfect positioning of Brisbane Water 'between wind and water'. 'To stand on

Killcare Heights,' he wrote, 'and to look across the cloud reflections in the waters where the little ferry to "the Woy" shuttles toylike through the misty alchemy of air and water, to hear the bellbirds chiming from the forest below and to see whirling in the clean clear air above the darting swifts and dollar-birds and sometimes a great sea eagle...this to me is the sublime bonus of the Australian scene.'

George also wrote of wild freesias and an overgrown little cemetery with 'tilted, hand-chiselled headstones of the 1820s' and stands of angophora 'as rose pink as the stones of Petra in the last light of day'.

'The Day of the Wombat', one of Charmian's newspaper essays from the 1960s, describes the Drysdale property as 'high and savage, old as the beginning of things, timbered with noble trees that curl their roots around the primeval basking rocks for want of soil for sustenance'. And on the day of a picnic, with everyone 'squatting around like some exotic tribe on a spreading shelf of rock hung out over the valley', the marvellous Maisie did indeed find a wombat for George and Charmian's youngest—via a local safari to Eric Worrell's Reptile Park.

I discovered the wombat piece in a Charmian Clift collection loaned to me by Maisie's neighbour, Sybil Medley. The place was marked by carbon copies of recipes for bean soup and dolmades typed by the late essayist. It has to be presumed she cooked them, with George, on their Greek island, perhaps tapping out

Mermaid Singing and *The Sponge Divers* on that very typewriter, rather inky in the upstairs of its lower case 'e'.

Down at the Bay, as we sit with our books and shandies in the late-afternoon, we like the idea of raising our glasses to the former librarian Maisie up on the hill as she enjoys a drop of white wine before the evening television news and plucks another book from her beautifully ordered collection. Plus toasts to those we wish we could have met—Tass, George and Charmian.

•

The tales of other settlers and visitors of note can be found amid the welter of information available from local historic societies and well-stocked libraries throughout Brisbane Water. While deep in research, I was thrilled to discover that the companion on my rail journeys, Phyllis Albina Bennett, was holder of Borrower's Card Number One at Gosford Library.

Visitors to the Coast can easily obtain a listing of the historic sites of the region, from pioneer cemeteries and early churches to the remains of a shipwreck at Maitland Bay between MacMasters Beach and Killcare. On May 6, 1898, the *Maitland* went down in a raging gale, broken clear in two. Twenty-six perished, nine of whom are buried in the little cemetery at Booker Bay, the waterfront suburb which coils under the southern pylons of the Rip Bridge. Its bell, salvaged in 1957, is displayed outside the one-time Maitland Store, now the ranger headquarters for the Bouddi National Park, staffed on weekends by volunteers ready to impart a wealth of local knowledge.

The master of Kirei and host to Sarah Bernhardt would doubtless have liked the fact that the Coast has a contemporary Japanese connection. Gosford has a sister city relationship with Edogawa and there's a commemorative garden at Caroline Bay with a tea-house, koi-filled ponds, cherry blossoms and raked-gravel gardens studded with stone lanterns. Blue heritage plaques have also started to spring up on Coast properties of merit, and a pleasant afternoon can be spent motoring in quest of listed cottages, boatsheds, one-time tearooms and shire halls. On the Bay's Araluen Drive, the little pink fibro house at Number 40 and its cream-and-green neighbour at Number 42 are heritage listed as built in 1922. A few doors down, the Old Killcare Store is circa 1920; black-and-white photos of the 1920s and 1930s show boatsheds, tracks for horses-and-carts and weekenders built on stilts in the style of Peacock Cottage.

Many Brisbane Water pioneers, and later residents such as Sir Russell Drysdale, are buried in the grounds of the tiny, ivy-shawled St Paul's Anglican Church at Kincumber. It was built in 1841 and has been classified by the National Trust; nearby, at Kincumber South, stands the Holy Cross Catholic Church, built in 1842 from locally quarried sandstone. It's also a classified building and it was to this congregation that Father

Cornelius Coughlan rowed in the 1840s from his lush banana plantation on what is now St Huberts Island.

Behind the Holy Cross Church stands what was once Kincumber Orphanage, a home for boys opened in 1887 and run by the Sisters of Saint Joseph, the holy order founded by Mary McKillop—the real Mother Mary of the Coast. She visited the orphanage on various occasions, at least once because a very ill boy had asked for her from his sickbed. Records show Mary McKillop made the journey five times in 1895.

After travelling by train from Sydney to Woy Woy, she would be rowed across Brisbane Water and up to Cockle Creek by the Orphanage's older boys, as she said rosary after rosary, always insistent the journey must continue, irrespective of the weather. An 'old boy' of the Orphanage, William McLeod, recording his impressions of the early days in John Dawes's historical record of Holy Cross, recalled that Mary McKillop had had a stroke. 'She was in a wheelchair and came on the train to Woy Woy. We chained her chair to a buggy and we went nine miles to the Orphanage. She was crying tears of joy as we walked by and kissed her hand. She was calling out "my children".'

In the final decade of its operation, girls were also admitted to the Home to create, as historic records rather sweepingly put it, 'a family atmosphere'. In 1976, remaining children were placed in foster homes with private families and the St Joseph's Retreat and Seminar Centre took its place—but old habits die hard on the

Coast, and locals still talk about the Orphanage as if it were alive and flourishing, with Mary McKillop handing out the boiled sweets she would bring up from Sydney for 'her boys'.

As well as producing fruit and vegetables and dairy goods from 1905 to 1960, the Orphanage ran a fleet of small ferries around Brisbane Water, delivering mail, newspapers and supplies to residents of the numerous bays and inlets. The service continued for a decade thereafter under a private operator, Stan Smith, until the 1972 opening of the Rip Bridge—'and the encroachment of the noisy jolting bus', as ferry-boat historian Graeme Andrews put it in 1969—connected settlements such as Kincumber, Empire Bay, Bensville, Killcare and our own Bay and peninsula with Woy Woy.

Graeme and I looked searchingly at pictures of these old Brisbane Water ferries, hoping to guess from which one Peacock Cottage's windows may have been recovered. Many of the boats had windows which opened up and down, rather than from side to side like ours. There's no way of being certain but in terms of shape and size, they could well be from one of the passenger ferries built to order for the Orphanage. As we slide the windows along, often needing to bang them for better manoeuvrability, we relish this tangible connection with the early Brisbane Water settlers and Mary McKillop's hard-working boys.

CHAPTER TEN

A River Runs Through

*Morning before sunrise, sheets of dark air
hang from nowhere in the sky
no stars there, only here is river.*

from 'Green Prawn Map' by Robert Adamson

Hawkesbury River–based poet Robert Adamson writes of the waterway's 'thousand winds' and its 'shoals and creeks, collapsed shacks'. An old skiff 'mutters, pushes up Hawkesbury mud' and the cast of a fishing rod flying out 'fine as spiderweb'. His partner, photographer Juno Gemes, produces haunting black-and-white images of fish caught in nets, tin-roofed shacks hugging the Hawkesbury shore, oyster farmers tending what Adamson describes as their 'tar-drenched racks'.

Northbound visitors to the Coast get their first look at the Hawkesbury as they zip across it, by train or car or, for a privileged few, by seaplane. But the whole point is to wander or hike its muscular shores and then actually get *on* it.

Brisbane Water National Park covers 12,000 hectares of 'rugged sandstone country', as the rangers put it. If visitors don't have a car, some Newcastle-bound trains stop at Wondabyne, past the Hawkesbury River Station, on the flatly named Mullet Creek. It can hardly be called a station: just a platform with a view. Alighting at Wondabyne has about it the air of safari as passengers must inform the guard in advance of their intention and they must ride, in bushwalker purdah, in the rear carriage as that's the only part of the train which pulls alongside the tiny platform.

From Wondabyne, there are two Great North Walk routes which split into various trails. For several weeks during the first summer of my regular rail commuting, there was a one-person tent pitched between the stone statues at the curious Sculpture Park near Wondabyne Station. A blond-headed backpacker flew the Swedish flag by his digs and some days could be seen pottering about like an exotic migratory bird amid a mini Stonehenge. Did he do Druid dances by moonlight? Phyllis Albina Bennett would have found a poem in it.

One doesn't need to be a hearty bushwalker to enjoy Brisbane Water National Park. Animal-spotting and wildflower-viewing reward those of gentler persuasion. There are waratahs in profusion during August and September and the flowering bells and bushes of Christmas display their oranges and scarlets in December. In the cool gorges are tree orchids, elkhorns and cabbage-tree palms. The rangers talk of swamp wallabies, koalas, echidnas, ring-tailed possums, yellow-bellied gliders and even shy platypuses as casually as one might describe the sighting of a sparrow.

•

The Hawkesbury Riverboat Postman departs from the Hawkesbury Marina each morning for a three-and-a-half-hour journey around this vitreous green waterway, snaking for 480 kilometres from its source at Crookwell to its entry into Broken Bay. Houseboats and cabin cruisers bump and bob around the blue-trimmed marina as the double-decker mail and supply service sets off.

The weekday morning of my tour, Captain Don was in command, his staccato commentary broadcast over the public address system as parties of tourists settled into position. The prime seats, on fine days, are those on the open top deck, but when morning tea is announced, there's a thundering rush downstairs for biscuits and cups of tea and coffee served in utility china of the stout government railways variety.

Past escarpments, tall and brooding, lusciously green in the shadows, the herbal colours of sage and rosemary in the strong sunlight. The river was known by the original Aboriginal tribe as Deerubben but was renamed by explorer Governor Phillip, we are told, after Lord Hawkesbury, President of Trade and Plantations in London. Sadly, it may not be an indigenous name but it's a good one, long and mellifluous and suggestive of birds.

There's one bend in the Hawkesbury known as Trollope Reach, so called because British writer Anthony Trollope visited in 1872 and grandly declared the river the equal of the fabled Rhine. 'The Hawkesbury has neither castles or islands,' he wrote, 'nor has it bright, clear water like the Rhine, but the headlands are higher, the bluffs are bolder, and the turns and manoeuvres of the course which the waters have made for themselves are grander, and to me more enchanting.' He also compared the Hawkesbury favourably to the Mississippi, with descriptions such as 'mysterious delight' appearing in his shapely sentences. In fact, Trollope appeared to be besotted with New South Wales. 'Inexpressibly lovely,' was his verdict on Sydney Harbour.

As we stopped at the landing for Little Wobby Camp, run by the New South Wales Department of Sport and Recreation as a youth lodge, immense boxes were passed across to a man on the shore by several crew members, one after another, in rapid relay style. There were big yellow plastic trays jammed with bread sufficient for several hundred sandwiches and cardboard cartons of various sizes. Empty crates came clattering on board. Goodbyes waved from aboard and ashore. The call of 'Line's away' and we were off.

Past Little Wobby Beach and Tumbledown, now served by electricity but still reliant on water services

such as ferries and taxi boats for a lifeline to the outside world. Next to Dangar Island—formerly the less prepossessing Mullet—where geese and ducks waddled a welcome. Bundles of the local newspaper were hefted ashore, a boy took collection of a bicycle, the Australia Post mailbag was particularly big and bulky for this drop. Gardens on Dangar Island are either tweezered or tousled, and architectural styles vary as much as Coastal streetscapes but all houses are angled for a view from their slender blocks backed by steep slopes.

Houseboats passed us by, trim and rather stately, not as ornamented as those from the days of Fairyland Boatshed when one rented *Loveland, Dreamland, Merryland* or *Lazyland*, banged away at the piano and idly hauled in those promised buckets of fish.

Under the Hawkesbury River Rail Bridge with its series of curved spans, like so many baked loaves. A parallel row of sandstone pylons once held the original Brooklyn Bridge but the material was too prone to cracking. Things got so bad at one stage, according to the electronically distorted spiel of Captain Don, that a railways employee used to have to sit aboard a skiff by pylon number four to check for further cracks as trains passed across, one at a time, restricted to travel no more than five miles per hour.

Beyond the corrugated shoreline, where the railway line curves its way toward Woy Woy, the trains disappear into the black cavities of stone tunnels as if they're wild beasts charging to their lairs. Past Long Island to the left and Spectacle Island to the right. Sandstone formations close to shore resemble honeycomb—huge chunks of Violet Crumble, textured enough to appear edible. Schnapper Rock looks like a giant version of its namesake fish, fat and formed with stony scales and lips. Under the Peats Ferry Bridge, opened in 1945 and now providing a scenic alternative to the 1972 freeway with its swooping lines, a real contrast to the clunky architecture of its predecessor.

As we stopped for a leg-stretch at the jetty for Camp Knox, run by Sydney's Knox Grammar School, life-jacketed lads rowed their canoes all around us, shrieking with glee while the water twinkled with sunlight. Recreational Nirvana for a sporty sub-teen.

'It's all so bewilderingly beautiful,' sighed the visitor from Cornwall with a touch of the Trollopes. His wife had leapt into action to help lay the buffet lunch for which an extra ticket needed to be bought. She bustled about with such vigour I wondered if she wasn't going to whip an apron out of her backpack. 'She's been away from home for three months,' he told me with a knowing wink. I was reminded of that old saying that the first thing a Cornishwoman does when she gets to heaven is to hang out a Bed and Breakfast sign.

The tables that had held postbags and boxes of groceries were now spread with cotton tablecloths checked in maroon and white. The ticket-holders hoed into coleslaw and curled luncheon meat, providing a chorus of clicking aluminium tongs for the commentary as we completed 60 kilometres aboard Australia's most unusual postal service.

With Captain Don at the helm, cold beers on sale via a servery hatch and the Cornishwoman clearing the dishes, there was never any chance the mail would not get through.

•

Graeme and I decided that to be considered real Bay people rather than those of the prissy parvenu kind, we really had to get out on the water. But we were too embarrassed to haul the Zodiac out of the garage. Graeme's sons, Jake and Barney, had taken charge of it when they were younger, zipping around Sydney Harbour like undersized but very fast expeditioners, but it had been languishing in a succession of sheds ever since.

About five years earlier, I had been yachting with a previous love interest and had botched things right up. I squelched about in my rope-soled canvas loafers with the cute gold anchors on the toes (bought for the occasion; women the world over do such things) and tried to find somewhere to sit where I wouldn't get a mark on my new white linen slacks, with matching blazer casually slung over my shoulder in the Côte d'Azur manner (so casually, in fact, it fell overboard). Then there was the matter of the toilet closet and its tricky pump. I soon decided kidney failure was preferable.

Added to all this discomfort were the barking orders from my man of the moment and the need to know one's port side from starboard without a second's dithering. Luckily, one of my schoolteachers had had us memorise a handy saying that goes: There's no port left in the sideboard. This worked a treat, enabling me to identify in an instant that port was the left side. Unfortunately, I got carried away with success and for no sound reason, jumped up and yelled, 'Keel to sideboard!'

Then there was my rebellious stomach. 'Six meals a day' used to be the offbeat promotional blurb for one yacht charter company. No, not oceans of food. 'Three down, three up' was the catch. It's never an insouciant look to board a boat mummified with anti-nausea patches and wearing the insignia T-shirt the chemist gave you when you purchased his entire supply of motion sickness medication.

Plus there's the matter of hair. Men who design and sail yachts invariably don't have any or else they would build in provision for the windproofing of same. All the strong-hold mousse in the world can't compete with Sydney Harbour or Bass Strait on a brisk day. Nor do they have any sense of humour, as I've found when suggesting I throw off a line and see whether it's lobster mornay or thermidor biting for tea. 'Silly boyish amusement...spending energies in aimless manner,' pronounced Mister Toad of *The Wind in the Willows*.

Graeme and I decided we would go public. On ferry boats, that is. We were intrigued by the Brisbane Water ferry culture and loved the toy tug feel of the Patonga to Palm Beach run. One morning we boarded the *Banksia*, a small ferry which does a regular service from the Woy Woy public wharf to Empire Bay via Saratoga and Davistown.

It's used by commuters and by sightseers who do the return run; in deference to the latter, the captain provides a commentary which crackles over one small loudspeaker. He sounds as if he's chewing gum in a tin can and is largely incomprehensible save for the word 'pelican' which he spits out from time to time when one of the big birds can be spotted on a jetty post. 'About as informative as a Marcel Marceau cassette,' whispered Graeme but his voice carried on the breeze and the couple from Auckland to my left heard him loud and clear.

The four of us collapsed in jolly, conspiratorial laughter as the commentary spluttered and the *Banksia* chuffed, slow and low, along the channel between the tangled nature reserve of Rileys Island and the manicured mansions of St Huberts. The contradictions between the two are extraordinary. On one side, all is green and wild and flocked with birds and, on the other, lawn sprinklers spray and canvas-awninged love-seats sway in the breeze.

Many of the water-frontage properties on St Huberts have private moorings and along one jetty, an owner has cultivated pots of petunias, placed side by side, in multi-coloured profusion, as one might decorate a VIP pathway to an official function. He was out and about in chief gardener mode the morning we passed by aboard the *Banksia*. A retired military man, we decided, as stiff-backed as a grenadier, with his plants standing to attention and, perhaps, just off stage, a rolled red carpet on standby for special arrivals.

The New Zealand couple were lively chatterers, enthralled with pelicans. Although I'd been convinced Ogden Nash was responsible for the pelican ditty I used to recite on school holidays, Sandra from Auckland was able to tell me it was Dixon Lanier Merritt and what's more she had a typed copy in her anorak pocket.

Who knows what the *Banksia*'s chewy-voiced captain thought as we pelican-fanciers formed a quartet and loudly launched into

> *A wonderful bird is the pelican*
> *His bill will hold more than his belican.*
> *He can take in his beak*
> *Enough for a week,*
> *But I'm damned if I see how the helican.*

•

In March, Phil entered his boat in the Putt Putt Regatta, an annual event in which 40 or so small boats with inboard motors make their way from Davistown to Woy Woy via the small islands, marine reserves and mangrove-lined channels of Brisbane Water. 'The gutter,' was how one crowd member described the slender passage between Rileys Island and St Huberts. I was standing across from him, half-hidden behind a tree, trying to take a picture of his T-shirt with its emblazoned message: 'My wife says I never listen to her—at least that's what I think she said.'

'Present from the wife,' he grinned, spotting me and posing, pulling the T-shirt taut over his barrel belly. 'We would never have guessed,' mumbled Graeme, who was trying to attract Phil's attention as he and Tim lined up their boat for the start. We'd had a vague plan to meet up and journey on board with them but now we were secretly pleased to be on shore as the rain was bucketing down. Phil's boat has its smart canopy top so all was reasonably dry aboard but those Putt Putt Regatta entrants in open boats were getting a right old drenching.

The regatta was revived in 1998 after a 35-year gap and looks set to be a yearly happening. Prizes galore for Best Boat, Best Costume and Best Overall Boat and Crew. Raffles to assist the Royal Volunteer Coastal Patrol (or 'floating Neighbourhood Watch', according to one ticket-seller). Entrants in straw boaters and braces, others costumed as flappers or first settlers. Members of a jazz band sitting in deckchairs on the back of a cabin cruiser. Two bachelors from Hardys Bay ('From Hardys Gay!' screeched an approving onlooker) in the most dapper of punting gear—blazers, bow-ties and striped jackets—lounging in their forest-green conveyance with scarlet trim as if about to be launched across the stage in a Noel Coward play.

The regatta was almost incidental to the occasion. Coasties never need much excuse for a shindig and therefore are great ones for local festivals. The marketing slogan 'special event tourism' may not have been coined to include such madnesses as the Top End's Barefoot Mud Crab Tying Competition or Stroud's International Brick and Rolling Pin Throwing Contest but such parochial festivals are important municipal money-spinners. They create a feeling of community bonhomie and proceeds usually aid a volunteer organisation, such as a bush fire brigade or coastal patrol.

Spending the day in this manner, eating sausage sandwiches and listening to a well-intentioned washboard player bravely soldiering on in the rain (the line dancers withdrew, due to wet grass and dripping cowboy hats), would have seemed inconceivable when we were still fortressed in suburban Sydney, where we never once celebrated any sense of neighbourhood.

CHAPTER ELEVEN
Bay of Plenty

'Have a pearler of a day!'

Slogan for the annual Oyster's Birthday, Woy Woy

There's more to Coastal cuisine than chiko rolls and fish and chips, although battered takeaways are available in abundance and no doubt still form the basis of many a holidaymaker's diet. It was a theme of cutlets and custard, if I recall correctly, at the Florida Guesthouse at Terrigal when Peggy and I holidayed with my parents all those years ago. Then, as now, ice cream vans prowled the pine-lined seafront avenues, with 'Greensleeves' crackling from their loudspeakers and soft-serve cones the special of the day. As a joke, my father once told me that if such vans were playing music, it was a signal they'd run out of ice cream. I announced this important fact to my schoolmates who giggled helplessly at such nonsense and it was quite some time, and many soft-serves later, that I finally forgave Dad for his trick.

Oyster farmers in the Brisbane Water region sell some 30 million of the plump, juicy specimens per year. Commercial fishermen supply premium flathead, whiting and bream; dipping a line into every bay and channel, there'll be a bunch of anglers, at it for hours, the jetty being the coastal equivalent of the garage or tool shed, the all-male domain. 'The hours spent in fishing are not deducted from a man's allotted span!' reads a poster in one local seafood shop, with attribution to Isaac Newton.

There are few better things in life, Graeme and I have decided, than Brisbane Water oysters squeezed with lime and showered with black pepper, then tossed down the throat while sitting at any of a dozen vantage points overlooking the Bay. There are public jetties at Pretty Beach and Wagstaffe as well as three at the Bay proper, where wooden steps provide the perfect perch for rest and contemplation. Someone from the Council has an appreciation of views, with benches and picnic tables angled at just the right position around the foreshores. How different from Hong Kong where civic seating has all been removed under the new Chinese rule for fear benches and tables could be turned to deadly missiles during riots.

Most houses at the Bay have barbecues, from little Hibachi-style grillers on decks to full industrial-looking numbers standing as potentate as altars in leafy backyards. One of the Woy Woy butchers sells 'pre-War sausages'—huge and runny with fat. On summer weekends, the air sizzles with good barbie smells and smoke. When Captain Cook first sighted the Central Coast of New South Wales in May, 1770, he reported 'smoak' from native fires. Phillip's journals reveal that the local tribespeople drank a sweetish concoction called 'bael', made by soaking banksia flowers in water. Aside from plentiful fish, they ate yams, native berries, fern roots and the heart of the cabbage tree palm.

We buy fish from Kevin and Barb Walters at MacMasters Beach. Theirs is a corner fish shop in the right sense of the word—they sell the day's catch from the garage of their corner-block home where the fridges and chopping block are wedged behind the family sedan. Silver bream, leatherjacket, schnapper, and prawns when their son, Mike, gets lucky. Buy the fish whole or Barb will expertly slice and fillet them on the spot. One late Saturday afternoon, we bought two filleted tarwine. 'How to cook them?' we asked. 'Fry 'em!' she laughed, so we did, putting aside all notion of Asian spices and clever sauces, and they were delicious, lightly coated with flour and served with home-made fat chips and salad, but all the more so because we'd bought them direct from the fisherman, as Bay people have done for decades.

•

The Oyster's Birthday is an annual festival which takes place on the first Saturday after Melbourne Cup and is held over a traffic-free zone on the Woy Woy waterfront, next to Fishermen's Wharf. Graeme and I ventured along, lured by that promise of 'a pearler of a day'. We expected cheap oysters and perhaps a glass of wine under the trees but were unprepared for such an exuberant air of fiesta.

Twelve thousand oysters were shucked open and sold. The Bayview Hotel had set up long tables under a shady arbour and sold Veuve Cliquot and boutique wines and beers by the glass. Bon vivants in straw hats mingled with fishermen and oyster farmers. There were sushi-making demonstrations, a mobile jazz band and myriad stalls selling just about everything fresh and edible, from herbs to Thai stir-fries.

'You'd kill for a nice bit of mullet,' said an old-timer as we queued for snacks of squid in chilli and coconut milk and fishcakes with lemongrass while the spanking fresh and green aroma of coriander hung in the air like deodoriser spray. 'They've come two to a horse today,' said his mate, surveying the big crowd.

'Lived in Woy Woy all your life?' I asked of the mullet man. 'Not yet,' he replied, leaning close, watery blue eyes creased with amusement at his cleverness.

The fishing fleet was blessed in an ecumenical service, the boats at their scrubbed-up and proudest best, multi-coloured bunting flying on masts and cabins. The festival was born in 1984 as a means of reviving the local oyster industry which had been affected by health scares, even though contamination actually had occurred with oysters from well outside Brisbane Water.

We ate a late and long lunch at Fishermen's Wharf that day, happy to idle away the afternoon, uncaring of an hour's wait for food to appear. 'Delays may occur due to the Oyster's Birthday,' warned a handwritten sign. And quite reasonable, too, we decided, on its once-a-year day.

•

We can't pretend there's a thriving restaurant culture at the Bay and environs but enough variety is on offer for us to eat out reasonably well. The Boathouse Bistro at the Hardys Bay RSL and Citizens' Club puts on a good show with its fish and chips and its wine at bar prices. Morosini's Cafe sometimes does excellent thin-crust pizza with various toppings on Sunday nights, but sometimes it's off the menu, and no one can predict when or why. Gandhi's Restaurant at Ettalong does very good Indian takeaway but we haven't eaten in, scared off, I must admit, by advertisements of the presence therein of 'Trevor, the Most Popular Entertainer on the Coast'. Whether Trev juggles pappadums or makes mango pickles disappear or just sings 'It's my Chappati and I'll Cry If I Want To', it'd take a braver reporter than me to find out.

The Old Killcare Store serves great coffee, which is an essential prop to modern life in our era when even laundromats and car-washes serve quick-fix espressos. Its mismatched tables and chairs are all rather rickety and rustic and it's full on weekends; I don't think we could have existed at some of the other pretty bays along the Coast, such as Phegans and Empire, where there's no cafe to repair to, newspaper under arm, for a fix of cappuccino society, even though our idea of dressing up to go out merely involves putting on shoes.

•

Hardys Bay Hot Stuff

Graeme Blundell and Susan Kurosawa

Serves 2

Ingredients

1 tablespoon peanut oil

1 leek, washed and chopped

1 brown onion, chopped

1 spring onion, chopped

4 cloves garlic, finely chopped

half a red capsicum, seeds removed, chopped

300 g green prawns, peeled and deveined; tails intact

1 bunch fresh coriander, washed, chopped

1 large red chilli, chopped

2 tablespoons Japanese-style soya sauce

1 tablespoon Indonesian sweet soya sauce ('ketjap manis')

lime wedges

Method

Heat the peanut oil in a wok (or large frying pan) over medium-high heat until oil is almost smoking.

Throw in leek, onion, spring onion and garlic and stir-fry for one minute.

Add red capsicum and stir-fry for 3 minutes.

Then add prawns, chilli and coriander (conserve some for garnish) and stir-fry for 2 minutes until the prawns just turn orange.

Add soya sauce and heat through.

Garnish with extra coriander and serve accompanied by steamed rice with lime wedges on the side to be squeezed over dish for extra zing.

Note: 'Ketjap manis' is available from Asian grocery stores and gourmet delis.

Black Mussels in a White Wine and Saffron Cream Sauce

Kims Beachside Retreat, Toowoon Bay

Serves 4 as entree, 2 as main course

Ingredients

2 tablespoons unsalted butter

1 onion, finely chopped

24 black mussels

2 cloves garlic

1 cup white wine

2 cups cream

2 teaspoons lemon juice

1 teaspoon saffron

2 sprigs of dill, finely chopped

seasonings to taste

Method

Heat butter gently and sauté garlic and onion with saffron.

Add mussels, wine and cream, place lid on top briefly until mussels open.

Remove mussels and keep warm.

Add lemon juice, dill and seasonings, reduce until slightly thickened.

Pour over mussels.

Serve with linguine or rice.

Manager Diana Kershaw advises that for many years, mussels for the famous buffet spreads at Kims were supplied by the legendary Clifford Fish Shop (now Jimbo's) at The Entrance, operated by Harry Clifford. 'Harry's father, Pat,' Diana explains, 'who's now in his nineties, would go to a "secret" location on Brisbane Water and harvest them especially for Kims.' But now the secret's out— it was Hardys Bay.

Fishermen's Wharf Kingfish

*Fishermen's Wharf Restaurant,
Woy Woy*

Serves 4

Ingredients

2.5 kg whole kingfish (ask your fishmonger to fillet, skin and bone)

1 tablespoon grated fresh ginger

1–2 teaspoons freshly chopped red chilli (to taste)

2 cloves chopped garlic

chopped coriander root

big handful chopped coriander

big handful finely chopped chives or spring onions

⅓ cup fresh lime or lemon juice

2 tablespoons fish sauce (available from Asian grocery stores)

⅓ cup light soy sauce

2 tablespoons brown rice vinegar

lime or lemon wedges

4 cups steamed jasmine rice and/or 500 g noodles, lightly stir-fried

Method

Combine chilli, garlic, coriander root, lime juice, fish sauce, soya sauce and vinegar (may be made up to a week ahead).

Barbecue the whole fillet of fish on a well-seasoned hotplate or fry it in a non-stick pan, using as little oil as possible. Kingfish cooks quickly and the flesh will turn white as it heats—test in thickest part with a knife.

Have rice and/or noodles ready and warm.

Place rice and/or noodles on a large platter and place cooked and cut fillets on top.

Scatter the fresh ginger and chilli, spring onions and chopped coriander on top.

Pour prepared dressing over the lot.

If more sauce is needed, top with extra squeezed lemon juice and soy sauce.

Serve immediately.

(Note: It doesn't matter if the dish loses a little heat as fish likes to 'rest' and the rice or noodles will soak up the kingfish juices and dressing.)

Fishermen's Wharf was the 1997 winner of the Sydney Fish Market's Best Fish and Chips in New South Wales Award and serves catches from 10 local fishing families plus the plumpest of Brisbane Water oysters. Owners Jenni Cregan and Merv Clayton are former Sydney finance journalists who took over the business, which includes an adjoining seafood market and takeaway shop, from Jenni's parents in 1988. Sydneysiders drive to Woy Woy especially for lunch here and Labor leader Kim Beazley chose it as a fuel stop during the 1998 Federal election campaign.

'Hardys Bay is blessed with a great variety of seafood,' says Jenni. 'All the favourites are found—luderick, jewfish, blackfish, silver bream, sand whiting and, if you travel beyond "the bowl", there's great schnapper and kingfish around the West Reef.'

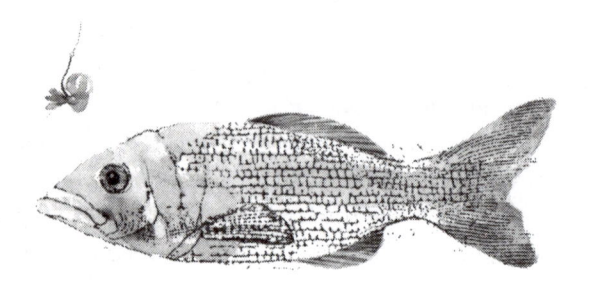

Kingfish is a Fishermen's Wharf favourite, according to Jenni. 'You need around 180 g per person of kingfish fillet for a good-sized meal. We find it criminal to do anything too fiddly with fish this fresh and tasty. We beg our fishermen to bring in local kingfish. It used to be less scarce when trapped but now it must be hand-lined and great kingfish brings big money on the auction floor, particularly for sushi.'

Jenni also has good tips on other varieties of fish. 'Don't throw away blackfish,' she says. 'They're delicious skinned, boned, then tossed in seasoned flour or deep fried. Blackfish are our favourite "fish piece" and can also substitute for redfish in recipes such as Thai fish cakes. Silver bream are often considered a poor second to schnapper but their flesh is even sweeter and they are delicious simply steamed in the microwave with a little soya sauce, lemon juice, ginger and shallots.'

Barbecued Bay Octopus

*Garry Deakes and Greg Scott,
Headlands*

Servings vary,
according to catch

Ingredients for marinade

1 x 400 ml can coconut cream (not milk)

2 tablespoons sweet chilli sauce

1 dessertspoon Indonesian sweet soy sauce ('ketjap manis')

1 tablespoon teriyaki marinade

grated zest of one lime

1 tablespoon finely chopped coriander leaves

½ teaspoon dried galangal

½ teaspoon dried lemongrass

1 dessertspoon palm sugar

½ teaspoon dried mango powder (optional)

Method

Blend above ingredients by hand for marinade and allow to stand.

Either purchase required amount of octopus at your preferred fish market or, in pure Bay style, Garry says wait until after nine on a moonlit summer's night and make your way by putt-putt to beneath the Rip Bridge. With torch in hand, wait patiently for octopus to surface and scoop up required amount.

At home, remove heads and pick out little black 'beaks'. Rinse and pat dry. If small enough, leave intact, otherwise cut tentacles into pairs of four.

Marinate for at least an hour.

Heat barbecue to very hot; drain octopus, reserving marinade, and cook until crispy.

Gently heat remaining marinade and spoon over plated 'occies'.

Home-cooked breakfast and multi-course dinner, expertly prepared by Garry, are included in the tariff at Headlands, the tiny retreat perched high over Pretty Beach. Attempts by Garry and Greg at organic self-sufficiency have been thwarted by rampaging brush turkeys, but they are well supplied with premium produce by local growers and regularly include Brisbane Water lobsters, octopus and oysters on the Headlands menus.

Nunn's Habit
Judy Nunn

Serves 4 as entree or 2 as main course

Ingredients

4 blue swimmer crabs (green, uncooked)

1 clove garlic, crushed

1 dessertspoon finely grated ginger

4 large shallots (or 8 small), chopped

1 tablespoon olive oil

2 tablespoons soy sauce

Method

Clean the crabs by taking off the top carapace and removing the spongy tissue beneath. Break the crab bodies in half and rinse clean.

In wok or frypan, fry the garlic in olive oil until aromatic flavour assails the nostrils. Add shallots and stir-fry briefly.

Add the crab pieces and put the top on the pan and allow to cook for 10 to 15 minutes, depending on size. Turn ingredients a couple of times. The dish is cooked when crab flesh is white and no longer transparent.

Add soy sauce, stir briefly.

To be eaten with the fingers.

Actor Judy Nunn describes her dish as 'messy but magnificent' and best served with chilled white wine. 'Blue swimmer crabs,' she advises, 'are inexpensive and readily available from Coast fish markets in season.' Judy and her husband, Bruce Venables, bought at the Bay in 1991 after spending their wedding anniversary at Headlands and falling in love with the area 'in an instant'.

'At Hardys Bay, I can return to the idyll of my childhood growing up on the Swan River in Perth by merely setting out in my dinghy and dropping a fishing line over the side,' Judy says.

Bay Oyster Soup
Paul Booth and Paul Arrowsmith

Serves 4

Ingredients

fish bones for stock
3 cups milk
2 cups fish stock or water
1 carrot, sliced
1 small brown onion, chopped
2 bay leaves
pinch of basil
4 peppercorns
salt, to taste
60 g butter
1 tablespoon flour
2 egg yolks, beaten
1 cup cream
2 dozen Brisbane Water oysters, on the shell
few drops Tabasco
1 teaspoon Worcestershire sauce
finely chopped parsley, for garnish
toasted croutons, for garnish

Method

Cut fish bones into small pieces and put into saucepan with milk, water (or extra fish stock), carrot, onion, bay leaves, basil, peppercorn and salt. Simmer gently for 30 minutes.

Strain and discard bones, vegetables and seasonings.

Melt the butter in a pan, stir in flour, add the strained fish stock, stir until boiling and cook for 3 to 5 minutes.

Beat together the egg yolks and cream, strain into the soup and stir over heat, without boiling.

Carefully remove oysters from the shell and place in mixture, add Tabasco and Worcestershire sauce and serve immediately so the oysters are just warmed through.

Garnish with parsley and serve with toasted croutons.

This recipe was passed on to Paul Arrowsmith by Alice Doyle, mother of renowned Sydney seafood restaurateur Peter, and it appears in a Doyle family cookbook. 'The soup takes some work and preparation,' say the Pauls, 'but it's well worth the effort.' Formerly of the Old Killcare Store, the two Pauls extol the 'excellence and succulence' of Brisbane Water oysters.

Marinated Sardines

David Farnham, The Galley

Allow five sardines
(or garfish fillets) per person

Ingredients (first step)

2 cups white wine vinegar
2 cups dry white wine
2 tablespoons brown sugar
2 cloves
4 bay leaves
10 black peppercorns
1 tablespoon sea salt

Method (first step)

Bring ingredients to boil in a non-reactive saucepan,
reduce for five minutes and allow to cool.

Ingredients (second step)

1 cup extra virgin olive oil
4 large brown onions, finely sliced
10 carrots, sliced on diagonal

10 garlic cloves, lightly bruised
handful of kalamata olives

Method (second step)

Cook onions over low heat until transparent.

Add carrots and garlic and continue heating until carrot is barely cooked through then add the prepared vinegar mixture.

Cook for a further 2 minutes and while still hot pour over prepared sardines or garfish fillets (see below) with olives. Refrigerate overnight for flavours to blend.

Either sardines or garfish fillets, lightly floured and pan fried, can be used for this dish. David suggests 5 butterflied fish per person, sprinkled with gremolata (garnish of finely chopped lemon zest and parsley; garlic can be added) and served at room temperature with sourdough crostinis.

Chef David Farnham of The Galley at Terrigal started his cooking career with Alex Herbert, including a stint at the Hardys Bay RSL Club in the heady days when the then Sydney Morning Herald *restaurant critic Leo Schofield discovered it, waxed lyrical and his readers descended by the carload. David lives at the Bay and is a true fan of its tranquil environment; he 'commutes' to Terrigal.*

Bouillabaisse de la Côte Centrale

André Chouvin, Café de la Gallerie

Servings vary, according to amount of seafood used

Ingredients

olive oil

½ fennel, diced

4 very red tomatoes, cut in quarters

4 garlic gloves

1 onion, diced

½ leek, diced

1 carrot, diced

1 bay leaf

1 thyme sprig

1 kg baby John Dory

1 kg red rock cod

1 tablespoon tomato paste

1 teaspoon saffron (optional)

Method

Pan-fry all ingredients, except fish, tomato paste and saffron, slowly with olive oil.

When all are soft, with no colour remaining, add fish and tomato paste.

Add sufficient water to cover and boil for 15 minutes to make a broth.

Add saffron and simmer for 20 minutes.

Pass through strainer or sieve to reveal as thick liquid. Return to saucepan and poach selected seafood in the broth—perhaps a few pieces of fish, prawns and mussels.

To prepare rouille sauce, make a paste with 50 g white bread and one garlic clove and add a pinch of paprika. Add one egg yolk and 1 g saffron (optional), then whisk in 2 tablespoons of olive oil to finish (should resemble a thick mayonnaise). Serve on the side in a jug, to be added to seafood after pouring on broth. Croutons, for garnish, can be made from toasted bread cut into squares.

bay of plenty 229

When I asked chef André Chouvin of Café de la Gallerie if he would contribute a 'local' recipe, he replied, 'Mais oui, but it will be French!' André's Australian wife, Tracey, explains he chose to give me this bouillabaisse recipe because it originates from the port of Marseilles. 'There are a lot of similarities between the French Riviera and "la côte centrale" in that lifestyle and food centre around the sea,' says Tracey.

André obtains seafood for his restaurant from Sydney and local sources—schnapper, for instance, comes from Terrigal. Café de la Gallerie is located at Kincumber in a casual, woodsy setting with deep green views of gums and ferns. The food? André was once apprenticed to various Michelin three-star maestros, including Paul Bocuse. In a word: magnifique!

Killcare Barbecued Teriyaki Kebabs

John McKinney

Servings: Allow 1 kg beef for every 4 persons

Ingredients for marinade

Japanese soya sauce
2 cloves garlic
knob of ginger, roughly thumb sized
sesame oil
sesame seeds
sugar (optional)

Method for marinade

In a suitable-sized container, place about a cupful of soya sauce to each kilo of beef.

Crush garlic and ginger and add to sauce.

In a large frying pan, heat sesame oil (enough to cover base of pan). Add sesame seeds to cover pan and heat until just turning colour.

Remove from heat and add to liquid.

Strength of marinade can be adjusted by adding water if too strong and a little sugar, if needed.

Method for beef

Several cuts are suitable, but beef should be free of any sinew (topside recommended).

Trim off all fat, cut into strips about 3 cm wide and stir into marinade.

Leave to marinate for at least four hours (overnight, if possible).

Before cooking, thread the beef strips onto individual skewers (metal or wetted wood), place into marinade container (with lid, for easy transport) in readiness for cooking over very hot barbecue. Serve with rice.

Architect John McKinney has lived at the Bay for 20 years but has also worked in Hawaii where this recipe was given to him by 'a foodie friend'. According to John, the McKinney clan ritual is to stake out a spot on Putty Beach in the late afternoon during summer and set up a picnic against the sandstone cliff. The cooking is done with a lightweight portable Hibachi and briquettes are used as fuel. 'They get hot enough to cook the kebabs quickly, which is essential,' says John. 'The sandstone cliffs heat up during the day and radiate warmth for hours after sunset, allowing us to stay well into the night—and the sunsets are wonderful from this viewpoint.'

John's final tip for this beach barbie dish with an Asian twist is to have the beef strips cut as thinly as possible: 'If you have a tame butcher, order the meat and ask for it to be lightly chilled and sliced by a bacon slicer.'

Fishy Business

These tips on safe handling of fish are from the Master Fish Merchants' Association of New South Wales:

- *If you know it will be a while before you get home after buying fish, take a small Esky or ice pack for the car.*

- *If fish has been in a plastic bag, unwrap it as soon as you get home and place in a glass or stainless steel dish. Cover lightly and keep in the coolest part of the refrigerator. Use as soon as possible.*

- *Don't allow water or ice to touch red fish such as tuna, trout or salmon or flesh will become discoloured.*

- *Always use a separate chopping board for preparing fresh fish and scrub with warm soapy water after use.*

- *If freezing fish, wrap fillets individually for ease of separation.*

- *Never thaw frozen fish at room temperature (always defrost in refrigerator or microwave) and never refreeze thawed fish.*

Jenni Cregan of Fishermen's Wharf, Woy Woy, has a final tip: 'The less handling the better with fish to maximise the moisture content.' As for those Brisbane Water oysters—leave on tray and cover with wet paper in coolest part of refrigerator. Will keep up to 4 days.

CHAPTER TWELVE
Travel, She Wrote

'I am now tired of drifting through other people's lives, tired of the intense activity and temporary friendships, tired of moving for the sake of the journey. I feel the need to stop travelling in order to absorb and understand what I've seen.'

from *In Rajasthan* by Royina Grewal

During this year of renovating Peacock Cottage, helping Graeme with the ambitious garden, entertaining guests and doing my desk work, I travelled on assignments to a succession of complicated places. Allowing just three days between, I flew back to Sydney from Chile and took off for Britain. I sat on a boat on the rain-lashed Norfolk Broads, feeding bread to sodden ducks with one hand and doodling designs for a day lounge for the new bedroom in the Peacock Cottage extension with the other. All the time trying to work out how 'SeaChange''s Laura Gibson managed to transform her Pearl Bay shack into a clever beach house with what appeared to be little more than a shell curtain, a lick of white paint and a few gaily draped shawls.

All of England to explore and I was cruising in East Anglia, wondering at the slowness and wetness of boating and why Ratty and Mole found it all so exhilarating. There were moments of pure joy, however, when ducks, quite fed up with the weather, hitch-hiked on the boat, huddled on its bow, grateful for someone else to be in charge of the getting there. Some countries, and England certainly is one, exist in the in-between places. Funny little villages give up their secrets more willingly than cities. You can only find England, China or Japan if you leave London, Beijing and Tokyo. So it is with the Bay: in modernised, multicultural Sydney, we could be almost anywhere on Earth, but the views from Peacock Cottage or Thistle Do, with their gums and kookaburras and fibro bungs, are so triumphantly Down Under you could transplant them into a snowdome or onto a tea-towel and sell them, no caption required, in an Australiana souvenir shop.

Not that this quintessential quality prevents me from looking for a sense of 'somewhere elseness'. The palmy end of Araluen Drive, towards Hardys Bay Parade, has the air of tropical North Queensland with its rainforest vegetation, high homes and mangrove swamps. The light-industrial strip at Blackwall looks unerringly like the outskirts of Fiji's Nadi or Vanuatu's Port Vila. Around Kariong, where the gum trees are dense and water views absent, the scenery is sheer Blue Mountains. There are snatches of New Zealand's Bay of Islands, the leafy green tunnels of Victoria's Dandenongs, the California coastline between San Francisco and Los Angeles, and the Hawaiian island of Kauai. Our cottage looks Caribbean, the garden is counterfeit Ubud.

Such fickleness of focus is the curse of the serial traveller.

•

Scenes from a darkened Istanbul hotel room: the sultry siren wriggled out of a feathery peignoir to reveal a lacy white bikini top and briefs. Tottering just a tad on black stilettos with heels like chopsticks, she pouted her cherry lips and crooked a come-hither finger. Music with shocking volume. Rap, rap, rap. MTV video clips, Turkish style.

I had been dozing but now sat bolt upright in bed and tried to turn down the TV with my tape recorder, the remote control having buried itself in the sheets during 'Larry King Live'. I am supposed to be an accomplished traveller but suffer the sort of jetlag fug and out-of-synch insomnia that even a slug of brandy and a sedative can't settle. I have become something of an uncelebrated expert on the quirks of international television. At two in the morning, from Santiago to southern Japan, there I'll be, pillow punching and channel surfing while trying to find a suitably soporific program to lull me to sleep.

In Turkey, quiz shows are loud and slapstick and arguably more entertaining when one doesn't have the faintest idea what's going on. The soap operas are easier to figure: boy meets girl, loses her, wins her back. Eternal themes, infernal clothes: boy has a bouffant that doesn't move, even when he's riding a horse in a three-piece suit en route to woo the village schoolteacher, herself a vision in Raggedy Anne plaits and torpedo bra.

When homesick, I channel hop in the hope of finding 'Home and Away'—so much more palatable when dubbed in a language I don't know. Usually end up with CNN 'News of the World'. Australia is rarely acknowledged as a part of the known universe but at least there may be a mention in the weather report. Comforting to know it's fine with a chance of cloud in Sydney; even the prospect of rain in Auckland is riveting compared with the American college basketball results.

Frequently, in India, after hours of early-morning sleeplessness, I have memorised the ads down pat. My all-time favourite is for VIP Frenchie Underwearings ('for the man who packs a punch') and I hum the jingle for weeks afterwards. Talk shows have for their guests a parade of pouty Bollywood starlets called things like Pinkie and Twinkle. When the giggling and eyelash-fluttering of the kohl-eyed sirens got too much one night, I rang the concierge in search of the hotel's advertised video service. A bellboy brought a VCR the size of a suitcase to my room and three maintenance men wandered in. They spent sufficient time to have rewired the hotel and loitered with noticing eyes in case the near-naked memsahib came slinking out of bed to administer a tip. Which I did, but my pink polka-dot pyjamas were not in the same class as Twinkle's bodice-heaving sari.

In Japan, instant addiction to television's late-night sumo world in which the blubbery wrestlers reveal irresistible details of their private lives, complete with close-up photography of their breakfast plates. Lots of riotous quiz shows with contestants lining up for electric shocks and pies in their faces and such holiday pastimes as being buried up to the neck in the hot black sands of Beppu with an army of ants let loose on their faces.

In Santiago, I couldn't get enough of something which roughly translated as 'Talking Animals'. Alas, no kookaburras, but Fluffy and Scruffy could have been headliners. Perfect for the wee hours: no need for subtitles or recall of my rusty childhood Spanish; just hours of cuddly cuteness as I snuggled down. From room service, warm milk and buttered white bread (I'd brought my own Vegemite, as ever). Fell asleep deeply while counting bambis. Uno, dos, tres, cuatro, cinco...

•

In August, my twentysomething 'baby', Joe, and I travelled to India with cricket legend Dennis Lillee so I could write for the *Australian* on the fast-bowling clinics Lillee conducts for young players in Madras, or Chennai as it's been renamed (although, like the

Bombay–Mumbai two-step, the old name continues to stick). Most afternoons were spent observing the amiable Lillee at his coaching sessions, surrounded by students like a holy sadhu with his followers. The God of Ball Things, as I dubbed him. Mornings were spent shopping. I had in mind a pair of Rajasthani wedding dolls and even though Madras, which is the capital of Tamil Nadu in the south, is a long way from Jaipur, Jodhpur and other such fabled cities of Rajasthan, I was determined to make the purchase.

As Joe and I trawled the streets for likely shops, we came upon a palm leaf reader, telling fortunes according to an age-old combination of astrology and interpreting Sanskrit predictions written centuries ago. Joe was told he'd marry a woman with a mole. Being in his mid-twenties and defiantly single, he retorted that he'd make sure he gave all women with moles a wide berth from then on. 'The mole,' hissed the fortune teller, leaning across the table and fixing Joe with eyes like black beads, 'will be in a secret place.'

At last I found the pair of wedding dolls, thereafter known as Rajah and Rani, standing as high as my waist, painted in glorious designs of pillar-box red and saffron. Together with some small pieces of furniture, I had the shop pack them into a crate to be shipped home. Sheaves of triplicate forms had to be filled in: India is the final resting place for the carbon paper supplies of this world, as Lillee was to find, too, when signing autographs. One night, a waiter at our hotel handed him a pad the size of a club sandwich, layered with carbon paper, for him to sign; apparently, the duplicate autographs could be readily sold on, with those on the faint side expertly touched up by this enterprising middle-man.

I had no doubt the Indian treasures would arrive safely; it was a reputable store and, despite the madness and muddle of the subcontinent, everything works in its own way. Once I had set off for a three-week trip around the south with no firm itinerary, simply someone's phone number written in pencil on a scrap of paper, handed to me at Sydney Airport by the Indian friend who was meant to be arranging my tour. Things worked out beautifully, although I did take the precaution of transferring the phone number into my contact book aboard the plane—firmly, in black ink.

Things started to deteriorate when the good ship *Bunga Teratai Satu* docked with my crate at Port Botany in Sydney and I entered an underworld of bureaucratic intransigence. It took a full day, starting before nine, to clear the goods, attend to matters of Customs and Quarantine and to pay a whopping amount of duty because the quaintly named Arts and Crafts Officer did not believe the goods were made by hand, which undoubtedly they were, India not being overrun with factories churning out wedding dolls. As I danced about and argued the point, I was told, with a smirk, that next time I should take photographs during the hand-crafting process as proof of my wild claims.

The quarantine officers asked me if I'd brought my own crowbar to open the crates. Tears seemed the only solution. As I wept and wailed, they took pity on me and assisted me onto the back of our ute, where they demonstrated the finer points of a crowbar while Graeme sat low in the front seat trying to look cool and detached, as if I were really just some deranged hitch-hiker he'd picked up.

It was afternoon peak hour as we drove from the surrealistic wastelands of Port Botany through the City and over the Sydney Harbour Bridge, headed toward the Coast. Rajah and Rani stood upright on the ute's tray, tied down with yellow rope, their faces set in rigid disapproval of such a bumpy and public passage from India.

In Istanbul, Christine and I trawled through the Grand Bazaar, buying up fabrics and bolster covers busily patterned with scenes of Ottoman battles. We sat on a balcony of our hotel, looking over the mighty Bosphorus and, beyond, shimmering in the lemony early-evening light like gold-leaf Byzantine miniatures, the spires of the Blue Mosque and the dome of Santa Sophia. I asked Christine, quite seriously, if she thought the Bay was more beautiful. 'In its own way,' she replied, with enviable diplomacy.

My suitcase began to weaken as I jammed into it Bay-bound booty from Japan, Hong Kong, Bali, Honolulu, Jamaica, Key West, Cozumel, Fiji and Tahiti. Two candle lanterns with battered brass tops and bottoms that I bought in Istanbul were hung on Thistle Do's deck on a trial basis, awaiting proper placement at Peacock Cottage. One night I walked around Araluen Drive until the vantage point was just right so I could look back at them, as bright as navigating lights across a channel the colour of medicine.

The next day I drove from the Bay to Sydney's international airport to board a plane for somewhere too far away and not half as beautiful and I fretted all the way, like a departing lover.

My life has been spent moving about and I realised I no longer knew what it was that spurred me on. At first, it had been intense curiosity, the need to know what lay out there, a continuum of my inter-continental childhood. At the age of three, Mother swept me aboard an ocean liner and we crossed the world. By five, my father had me by my gloved hand, off on expeditions by train to London and to the sea, to teach me 'the art of observation'. In our family, standing still for too long in one place showed an intolerable lack of imagination and purpose.

Flaubert wrote that travel makes one see 'what a tiny place one occupies in the world'. My constant journeys constantly taught me who I was. I understood my frailties, shortcomings, levels of tolerance and endurance in a way I would never have tested if I'd stayed at home. As a media ambassador for the refugee aid organisation Austcare, I visited camps on the border between Thailand and Burma and in Eritrea. I travelled with big, bearded doctors from Médécins sans Frontières and saw landmine victims waiting to be fitted with artificial limbs and women giving birth in ricefields. I slept in bamboo huts and washed in jungle streams, I held orphaned babies, I learned to travel with a backpack not much bigger than my handbag and I felt liberated and light-headed at my lack of encumbrance.

I'd return home, restless and impatient with the small complaints of my friends and family. I forced my sons onto planes and pushed their holidays beyond resorts and theme parks. We were Gypsy-like in our nomadism. To stay still was to be bored and boredom was as bad as death. We didn't change cities but we moved around Sydney so regularly that I may as well have opened a monthly account with the ever-patient Karel at Fast Movers. We tried the silvertail suburbs, the working-man's inner-west, the harbour-view strand and the heights of Bondi Beach. Justin and Joe took it in their stride and, come holiday time, boarded planes with casual coolness. They thought it perfectly normal to tell their teacher that Mummy couldn't do canteen duty because she was in Patagonia that week. At age five, Justin announced to his class in Show and Tell that his mother's job was writing in planes.

But now the need for trespass was diminishing. I had finally put down roots and, like Indian writer Royina Grewal, I was fatigued by the temporary and falsely intimate relationships forged by my unceasing travels. It was time to take stock, and Graeme was my touchstone.

While writing this book, I read an obituary in *The Times* of Iris Murdoch, the Booker Prize-winning novelist and philosopher, who had married John Bayley, a professor of English at Oxford University, in 1956. 'Together,' according to the obituarist, 'they lived a life of cosy intellectual companionship, haphazard domestic arrangements and culinary creations.' It sounded so much like Graeme and myself that I shed a tear. Our endless chatter, my casual regard for housekeeping, his obsession for cooking. At last, the little girl who'd been trained for a life of movement and observation just wanted to stay put and relish the lot.

•

This feeling of travel lag came and went in waves. My job demanded assignments beyond my desk. I scaled down the frequency but I couldn't refuse to stop flying altogether. But travelling with Graeme, who has journeyed very little, lessened my unaccustomed homesickness. In September, we met in Hong Kong. He'd flown from Sydney, I was returning from Istanbul. It was his first visit, my thirty-fifth. I sat on the Star Ferry from Kowloon to Hong Kong Island wondering how I must have felt on that first crossing, in 1968. Thirty years later, it was a journey so familiar that I failed to be entranced by the rebelliously fast water traffic and, beyond, the CBD skyline, all radiant and spiky, with buildings topped by spires so thrusting they are variously known by locals as the Chopsticks and the Hypodermic.

The ride lasted just five minutes and Graeme provided a running commentary. He pointed to a junk. Excited, camera out. Batwing sails the colour of oxblood, high prow of the sort on which pirates would perch, telescope trained to a distant horizon. That's a sampan, I told him, playing along, as a little wooden boat was tossed about in the wake of a passing container ship. He held onto my sleeve, like a child, as I moved off into the crowd. I sensed his fear at being lost but it gave me no thrill of superiority to be the one who already knew it all.

His sense of wonderment continued for days as we did Hong Kong upside down, inside out. I had the maps and the different dollars and the sense of direction and he had the camera, the ceaseless questions and the shopping list. Day One passed with an edge of tension as he quizzed me on the bleeding obvious. But by Day Two I was acting like a tourist again and seeing things anew, with him, through the noticing eyes of a novice visitor. His rapture was infectious. We breakfasted on yum cha at the Luk Yu teahouse on Hong Kong Island. The decor is Hong Kong circa 1920 with hard cherrywood chairs, brass spittoons on the floor and pyjama-jacketed waitresses slopping tea from big metal pots. He told me they looked like roving midwives just as one produced a towel and came at me with a kettle. I snapped shut my legs and we collapsed in great gusts of laughter.

Couldn't keep him off that harbour. By ferry, again, to Sok Kwu Wan on Lamma Island for a seafood dinner.

Dusk became inky night as we sailed past the western shores of the island. The filing-cabinet-style apartment blocks appear so romantic when their windows are defined as lozenges of light and you can't see their boxiness, shabby cement and sad lack of personality.

'Like extravagant pins in a cushion already overplanted,' wrote Henry James of New York skyscrapers. The description equally applies to the vertical streetscape of Hong Kong. As the ferry buzzed by, we renamed one with many twinkling windows as the Glomesh Bag, delighted to have appropriated a Hong Kong building as our own.

Despite the pretentious title of the Genuine Hilton Seafood Restaurant, and the lack of local impostor Hiltons intent on stealing its crown, we chose it for a bumper feed of Lamma's freshest. Mounds of prawns coated with salt and pepper, a cracked crab in black bean sauce and a pyramid of chlorophyll-green Chinese vegetables, as crunchy as crackers. The restaurant was near empty and we sat, the two of us, at a round table for 10, and sent the Lazy Susan spinning as if it were a quiz-show wheel of fortune. Not that such things are known as Lazy Susans chez Kurosawa; instead, they have been renamed Lazy Doreens. My apologies to the Doreens of this world, but this Susan has more than had her fill.

We took a dip at Repulse Bay Beach, shoulder to shoulder with the Sunday crowds. A galaxy removed from Putty Beach, we decided, and certainly the first time Graeme had been swimming standing up. At Stanley Markets, a seafront strand of stalls and hawkers, we bought matching hot-water bottle covers in Chinese silk, printed with the classic willow pattern. (A week later we were using them at Thistle Do after the combustion heater door blew off, covering Rajah and Rani with a fine film of ash and leaving the house like an ice cube.)

By Day Three, Hong Kong felt like a place I had never visited before. We did every corny thing imaginable, from fighting for the front seats on the Peak Tram and the Repulse Bay bus to taking photos of each other in the lobby lounge of the Peninsula, little fingers crooked as we drank Mr Twining's finest. In our room, we watched Jackie Chan videos and screamed with delight at the resonance of seeing the martial arts comic high-kicking his way around Hong Kong while the city was framed like a postcard in the window.

Graeme told me that I was a great tour guide as our interlude came to a close. He hoped I wasn't bored. I told him how grateful I was to see a familiar city through refreshed eyes. I made a promise to myself that no matter what shortcomings I may be accused of as a traveller, I will not let boredom and indifference figure among them.

•

While leaving the Bay was emotional, sometimes we had practical fears about absence. During the summer of

1997–98, close to 6000 bush and grass fires were reported in Sydney and on the Coast. We were afraid to drive to Sydney, convinced that Peacock Cottage would be gone when we returned, with Alfredo neatly kippered.

The cottage is surrounded by eucalypts, trees known to explode under intense heat, but they're so elemental to the Bay it would have been unthinkable to cut them down. Graeme had planted such slow-to-burn natives as brush box, lilly pilly and kurrajong. Succulent groundcover had spread every which way; between December and April, we kept plastic buckets and the laundry tub permanently filled with water.

Checking and cleaning gutters and downpipes had become as regular a task as sweeping the front step was during our city incarnation. Firebreaks had been cleared behind the cottage and a kit of full-sleeved shirts, long pants, goggles, heavy footwear and torch was on permanent standby.

Neither of us has had any dangerously close calls with fires, although Graeme loves to recount my story of driving to visit Frank and Jill Mullens at their Mount Wilson estate in the Blue Mountains one fire-prone Sydney summer. I was in my Capri convertible, top down, and in the passenger seat was a huge toy gorilla I'd won in a travel raffle. Urban, as he was inevitably called, was dressed in sunglasses and a baseball cap, strapped with a safety belt, and on his way to visit an identical gorilla which Jill kept in the mountains. I was turned back by billowing smoke on the Bell's Line of Road by a strapping policeman who took one look at what appeared to be a small, scorched passenger and declared, 'Take him home. I think he's had enough heat for one day.'

Garry and Greg up at Headlands claim their Bay baptism was by fire. While clearing the property just before they built, they did some burning off, not realising that it's mandatory to alert the local bush brigade if a fire is to be lit. They hadn't put in their steep driveway up from Pretty Beach at that stage so access was via fire trails along the ridge and, sure enough, within half an hour of the first smoke being sighted the volunteer brigade had arrived. Garry and Greg were mortified, already keenly aware that some locals with suspicions about the Bacchanalian goings-on at 'an exclusive retreat' referred to them as 'those poofters on the hill'. But things were soon smoothed out and it was cups of tea all round before the fire engine trundled off.

•

Of more concern this past summer, with heavy tropical rain staving off coastal fires, has been the record number of drownings on New South Wales beaches. Some swimmers have been fortunate: at Ocean Beach, Umina, two youngsters were saved by a quick-thinking lifesaver; occupants were rescued from a half-cabin cruiser washed onto rocks at Little Ladder Beach, near Box Head. More than 7000 people a day flock to Avoca in summer and almost as many to Terrigal; six surf rescues per day at each is the norm. The sign at MacMasters Beach may say 'Closed' but still they swim; at Putty Beach, the safety flags were so close together one day that the swimmable defile was barely as wide as six bodies shoulder-to-shoulder.

Two young girls, Elsie 'Biddy' Bowcock and Beryl West, were drowned at Avoca Beach on December 30, 1928. Beryl's body was never recovered but Biddy's body lies in the cemetery of St Paul's at Kincumber. It was this tragedy that hastened the formation of the Avoca Beach Surf Life Saving Club, still a mighty presence on the Coast.

By early February, when the Summer People had vanished, I could walk along Putty Beach again and pretend it was my very own. Everyone calls it Killcare Beach, or Killy, but officially it's Putty Beach, with Killcare the name of the residential district—or the 'ocean village' as scenic brochures and real-estate agents insist. One high-sky Monday noon, I was the only person on the beach. At the southern end, I dipped my feet in rockpools washed by the waves. The water fizzes so beautifully that my friend Jill calls them 'lemonade lagoons'. Parents sit their toddlers in the pools and the little ones squeal with delight at the bubbles and the foam.

A seagull joined me for a stroll that morning, its little feet leaving a pattern like arrowheads. When the waves came in, it stepped back, daintily, like a Victorian lady afraid of getting her feet wet. 'Silly seagulls' was how Ogden Nash dismissively described them. Graeme and I saw a seagull trying to eat an aluminium can on Thistle Do's jetty one day. I was reminded of the Guinness Book of Records champion, Monsieur Mangetout, who ate 10 bicycles, eight television sets and a Cessna light aircraft. Nothing silly in that if you make a splendid international career out of it and don't, literally, bust your gut. The seagull on the jetty gave up on its can but I like the way these much-maligned birds just get on with things, so shameless but yet so conscientious in their scavenging.

Since we moved to the Bay, various changes have occurred—only small interruptions but ripples can feel like tidal waves in a community this small. Adam and Ellen have had a daughter, Mia, a sister to Max. The two Pauls have given up the Old Killcare Store but they still live in their hilltop eyrie, enjoying a sabbatical from early-morning starts and the loud urgency of the Summer People. Mother Mary has moved into a new home where all is cool and creamy, from tiles to cement-rendered walls. She burns big candles and floats about in white dresses and looks like a barefoot temple maiden, albeit one with a voice loud enough to call home her Joe and Dylan from the Yum Yum tree.

The custard-coloured townhouse development on Araluen Drive that was built midway through the year, much to the horror of those of us committed to the shack vernacular, has been softened by the pom poms of crepe myrtle bushes, as pink as showground fairy-floss. The broad-leafed shrubs planted as instant landscaping in this stockade's pocket-hankie gardens have flourished this wet, tropical summer, but rumours abound about the resident 'townies' cutting back the mangroves on the opposite shore for a better Bay view.

The local progress society has been busy with placards and pickets against another medium-density development around at Wagstaffe. We sign petitions with a firm flourish, happy to have been so warmly welcomed into the bosom of the Bay. People wave to us wherever we walk. The Yum Yum tree drinkers salute with their cans and Graeme doffs his gritty old baseball cap.

As I write this, rumours abound that Tom Cruise and Nicole Kidman are buying a chunk of wooded peninsula. The director John Woo supposedly is looking for Bay sites for his latest action movie. 'He could start by blowing up a few of those boats,' remarked a

Yum Yum tree regular, waving his can toward a couple of very flash cabin cruisers.

There's talk of the little Woy Woy Library being renamed in honour of Woy Woy boy made good Spike Milligan, and it's been reported that the legendary Goon is 'quite delighted' at the prospect. The Wagstaffe General Store still has a handwritten notice in its window for a lost chook—'Very friendly. Answers to the name of Tina'. We continue to talk about hauling the Zodiac down to Hardys Bay Marina and getting the motor in working order. The public toilet block beside the Yum Yum tree has been painted a sage green with a very neat stencilled frieze of ferns—not the work of Gosford City Council but heritage bandits intent on the gentrification of the bay. One day rugged old red brick and, overnight, a magical change to bushland baroque. It's an ironic reversal to the more usual urban graffiti.

Justin has taken a high-flying hotel management job in Melbourne and Joe is overseas again, working as a teacher and no doubt learning how to say 'mole' in a variety of languages. We have sold the warehouse apartment in Surry Hills in readiness to make Peacock Cottage Phase Two our permanent home. The umbilical cord to the metropolis that was once the glittering centre of our universe has been chopped.

With the transplantation of our city chattels, Thistle Do is now packed to the gunnels with so many arrangements that when little Sebastian last came for a visit, he asked me why we were living in a shop. But there's room to move if we don't practise star jumps, and Rani and Rajah are guarding the books and the Indian and Indonesian and Turkish artefacts in preparation for our imminent passage across the Bay. And we are thrilled to have discovered a piece of music, 'Letter from Hardys Bay', composed for piano and strings by Nigel Butterley. I plan to track it down to use as Peacock Cottage's theme with Alfredo providing his emphatic accompaniment from somewhere off stage.

Andrew Strachan from Kims at Toowoon Bay has rung to tell me he's earmarked one of the resort's baby peahens as a partner for Alfredo and some time soon we can expect a visit. I'm hopeful she will find Alfredo to be 'a suitable boy' and that Andrew's role of arranged marriage broker will not have been in vain. If a male offspring should arrive, I already have the name—Clive. As in Clive Peacock of the ABC-TV mini-series 'The Missing Postman'. And with a bow to Clive of India, naturally. Graeme refuses to comment on my continuing lunacy but Eduardo the Chilean painter, who can't quite follow the thread of my name associations, nevertheless approves of my passion for the project and hopes Alfredo will be happy with his new 'missus postman'.

Whether or not the peafowl pair do hit it off, there'll be plenty of extra platform space for Alfredo to perform his disco tail dancing as the plans to extend Peacock Cottage have all been approved and a portion of the cliff, neatly angled between the trees, is now excavated for Michael and his team of tradies to start work.

Michael refers to the timber addition as the Shed on Legs. I go all ladylike and tell him it's Peacock Pavilion. Graeme calls it the Shack at the Back.

Life at the Bay flows on.

The Road Ahead?

Tens of thousands of people commute to and from the Coast to Sydney each weekday and thousands more make trips for casual visits. As I write, it appears plans have been approved, despite vocal opposition from Coast residents, for a 450-passenger Fast Ferry to make six round-trips a day from Ettalong to Sydney's Circular Quay. Around 600 tourists are expected to take advantage of the 40-minute service each day. A 228-room seven-storey resort hotel and casino complex is proposed for Ettalong.

The upside is that the international development will create much-needed jobs, but the depressing factor is that the Coast's special Aussie charm could be lost forever. Hawkesbury River residents have similar fears, with a three-stage resort development rumoured to be in the pipeline for Kangaroo Point.

The name Ettalong means 'place of drinking' in an Aboriginal dialect but its first uncharted name was Bar Swamp. A reference to sand bars, no doubt, but perhaps the progress from billabongs to resorts with swim-up bars always has been inevitable.

Bibliography

A Net of Fireflies by Harold Stewart, Charles E. Tuttle, 1960

'Are we there yet, Dad?' by Paul Dyer from *Places in the Heart* edited by Susan Kurosawa, Sceptre, 1997

Bouddi Peninsula Study edited by Beryl Strom, Association for Environmental Education, Central Coast Region, 1986

Collected Verse from 1929 On by Ogden Nash, J.M. Dent & Sons, 1961

Enchanted Waters by Charles Swancott, Brisbane Water Historical Society, 1961

'Endangered Spaces' by James Cockington, 'Domain', *Sydney Morning Herald*, December 28, 1998

Field Guide to the Birds of Australia by Ken Simpson and Nicolas Day, Viking O'Neil, 1989

George Johnston: A Biography by Gary Kinnane, Nelson, 1986

Good Old Woy Woy by Charles Swancott, Brisbane Water Historical Society, 1968

Gosford and Central Coast Sketchbook by Ronald Revitt and Beryl Strom, Rigby, 1980

Gosford and the Kendall Country by Charles Swancott, Brisbane Water Historical Society, 1966

Gosford/Wyong History and Heritage by Beryl Strom, Gosford District Historical Research and Heritage Association, 1982

Hawkesbury River Saga by Charles Swancott, Brisbane Water Historical Society, 1967

Images in Aspic by Charmian Clift, Horwitz, 1965

In Rajasthan by Royina Grewal, Lonely Planet Journeys, 1997

Kangaroo by D.H. Lawrence, Thomas Seltzer, 1923

MacMasters Beach—A History by Beryl Strom, Gosford District Historical and Heritage Association, 1985

'Manhattan Transfer' by James Langton, 'Good Weekend', *Sydney Morning Herald/The Age*, August 15, 1998

Mugal India: Splendours of the Peacock Throne by Valerie Berinstain, Thames & Hudson, 1997

'My Idyllic Childhood Summers' by Tim Winton, *Sun-Herald*, January 3, 1999

Old Gosford and District Album by Gwen Dundon, G.M. Dundon, 1985

Patonga and Some of Its People by Ben Smith, Leisure Publications, 1990

'Peacock's Pointless Plumage' by Graeme Phillips, *Sunday Telegraph*, September 20, 1998

Place Names of the Central Coast by Eileen Pratt, Brisbane Water Historical Society, 1978

Poems by Phyllis Albina Bennett, self-published

Summer People by Janice Elliott, Hodder and Stoughton, 1980

The Bodysurfers by Robert Drewe, James Fraser, 1983

The Central Coast: The Shires of Gosford and Wyong edited by Paul Ife Horne, Today Publications, 1968

The Clean Dark: Poems by Robert Adamson, Paper Bark Press, 1989

The Ferries of Sydney by Graeme Andrews, Trident, 1969

'The Shack in the SA Unconscious' by Kerryn Goldsworthy, *Adelaide Review*, January 1999

Towards the Future by John Dawes, The Holy Cross Church, South Kincumber, 1992

Why...and Later by E.A. Poole, Avoca Beach Surf Life Saving Club, 1979

Women of the Central Coast, Part One, Brisbane Water Historical Society, 1988

Women of the Central Coast, Part Two, Brisbane Water Historical Society, 1990

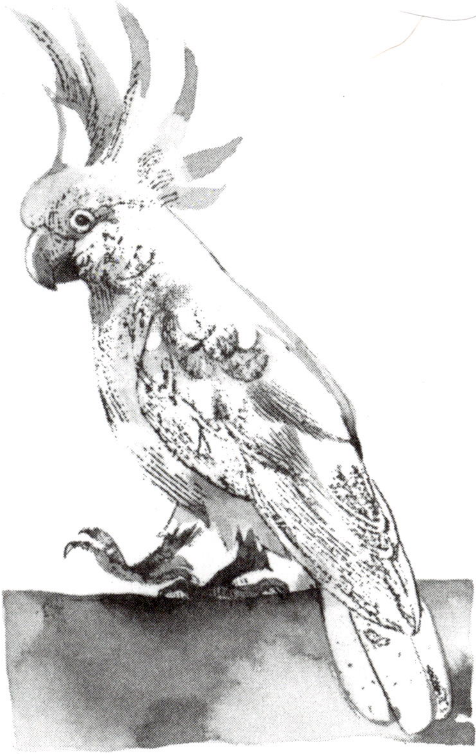